PRAISE FOR
SATAN'S SECRETS EXPOSED

Satan would like nothing better than to keep you from putting on the whole armor of God. And he not only uses special tactics to make you relax your guard, but he's also a very smooth liar and can deceive you into believing he has no power in your life. *Satan's Secrets Exposed* will help you resist the temptation to become complacent about the state of your walk with the Lord.

BISHOP CHARLES BLAKE
WEST ANGELES CHURCH OF GOD IN CHRIST
LOS ANGELES, CALIFORNIA

God has graced Dr. Fletcher with the insight and anointing to shine light on the underground works of the prince of darkness. Reading this powerful exposé will declare the Body of Christ cognizant of the deceptive maneuvers and tricks of Satan. *Satan's Secrets Exposed* most definitely has the potential to be an effective and timely weapon in the hand of every believer.

PASTOR DARRELL L. HINES
CHRISTIAN FAITH FELLOWSHIP CHURCH
MILWAUKEE, WISCONSIN

Dr. Fletcher closely examines spiritual warfare and why most believers pretend the enemy doesn't exist. Dr. Fletcher exposes the deception and gives readers the weapons to combat the enemy. I highly recommend *Satan's Secrets Exposed*.

LARRY JONES
FOUNDER AND PRESIDENT, FEED THE CHILDREN
OKLAHOMA CITY, OKLAHOMA

In the art of war it is known by all the great generals of history that the key to victory is the study and understanding of your enemy. Knowledge of your adversary, his strengths, weaknesses and proposed plans is vital to developing effective strategy for holding the advantage.

The Bible is clear that we as humans are engaged in spiritual warfare and must be trained, knowledgeable and skillful in use of our spiritual weapons. Our spiritual adversary, Satan, capitalizes on our ignorance, and therefore we are admonished not to be ignorant of his devices. In this standard-setting book, Dr. Kingsley Fletcher reveals the strategies of Satan in such a graphic way that anyone who reads can become an expert in recognizing and defeating this unemployed cherub. I encourage everyone to peal these pages for wisdom destined to expose the weakness of Satan. This book is a classic and should be in the library of every serious student of the Bible.

DR. MYLES MUNROE
BAHAMAS FAITH MINISTRIES INTERNATIONAL
NASSAU, BAHAMAS

Kingsley Fletcher knows that Satan fears informed believers. That's why he has written this fearless exposé. Dr. Fletcher reveals the enemy's diabolical strategies and empowers Christians with the tools of victory. If you want to see the devil defeated in your life, this is the book for you!

DUTCH SHEETS
SENIOR PASTOR, SPRINGS HARVEST FELLOWSHIP
AUTHOR, *INTERCESSORY PRAYER*
COLORADO SPRINGS, COLORADO

Dr. Fletcher exposes many of Satan's lies and does it in such a skillful way, he captures your attention from the first page to the last. He uncovers the devil's tactics with Bible scriptures and interesting illustrations. His encouraging book challenges the reader to make a decision: give in to the enemy or battle to victory with weapons Christ has provided. I hope you'll share this book with friends who need it, as I plan to do.

QUIN SHERRER
AUTHOR, *PRAYING PRODIGALS HOME*
COLORADO SPRINGS, COLORADO

Dr. Kingsley Fletcher has done a great service for today's Christians who are bombarded with misinformation about Satan and his activities. *Satan's Secrets Exposed* does just that—it exposes Satan for who he really is and uncovers his deceptions. Dr. Fletcher communicates profound spiritual insight, which is firmly rooted in Scripture, in simple and easy-to-understand terms. *Satan's Secrets Exposed* has opened my eyes to this often ignored yet enormously important dimension of spiritual understanding concerning the enemy. I have no doubt that everyone who reads this book will come away with a fresh understanding and appreciation for our spiritual battle against Satan and become better equipped to discern his activities of deception.

REV. DR. TERRY YAE
EMMAUS MISSION CHURCH
CLOSTER, NEW JERSEY

SATAN'S SECRETS EXPOSED

KINGSLEY FLETCHER

Regal

From Gospel Light
Ventura, California, U.S.A.

Published by Regal Books
Gospel Light
Ventura, California, U.S.A.
Printed in the U.S.A.

Regal Books is a ministry of Gospel Light, an evangelical Christian publisher dedicated to serving the local church. We believe God's vision for Gospel Light is to provide church leaders with biblical, user-friendly materials that will help them evangelize, disciple and minister to children, youth and families.

It is our prayer that this Regal book will help you discover biblical truth for your own life and help you meet the needs of others. May God richly bless you.

For a free catalog of resources from Regal Books/Gospel Light, please call your Christian supplier or contact us at 1-800-4-GOSPEL *or* www.regalbooks.com.

Originally published as *If I Were Satan,* Destiny Image, 1991.

Cover and Interior Design by Robert Williams
Revised edition edited by Kyle Duncan

LIBRARY OF CONGRESS CATALOGING-IN-PUBLICATION DATA
(Applied for)

1 2 3 4 5 6 7 8 9 10 11 12 13 14 15 / 09 08 07 06 05 04 03 02 01

Rights for publishing this book in other languages are contracted by Gospel Literature International (GLINT). GLINT also provides technical help for the adaptation, translation and publishing of Bible study resources and books in scores of languages worldwide. For further information, contact GLINT, P.O. Box 4060, Ontario, CA 91761-1003, U.S.A. You may also send e-mail to Glintint@aol.com, or visit their website at www.glint.org.

Finally, be strong in the Lord and in his mighty power. Put on the

full armor of God so that you can take your stand against the

devil's schemes. For our struggle is not against flesh and blood, but

against the rulers, against the authorities, against the powers of this

dark world and against the spiritual forces of evil in the heavenly

realms. Therefore put on the full armor of God, so that when the

day of evil comes, you may be able to stand your ground, and

after you have done everything, to stand. Stand firm then, with the

belt of truth buckled around your waist, with the breastplate of

righteousness in place, and with your feet fitted with the readiness

that comes from the gospel of peace. In addition to all this, take up

the shield of faith, with which you can extinguish all the flaming

arrows of the evil one. Take the helmet of salvation and the sword

of the Spirit, which is the word of God (Eph. 6:10-17).

DEDICATION

I dedicate this book to

the glory of the Lord;

*my wife, Martha, who has been a tremendous
strength to me in the ministry;*

all those who need victory over Satan's works.

CONTENTS

Part III: Your Weapons and Your Decision

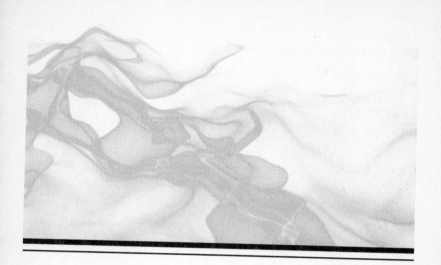

INTRODUCTION

I was born and raised in the West African nation of Ghana. Through the centuries many explorers and historians have referred to Africa as the "dark continent." However, for me, growing up as a boy, I learned about the wonderful Light of the world—Jesus. Because of my Christian upbringing, I received the grace of God early in my life. As a result, today I am experiencing His continuous blessings. I can say that I am not going under; I am going over. I am not defeated; I am victorious. I am not a loser; I am a winner. I do not dwell in darkness; I rejoice in the light.

Throughout its history, much of Africa has been given over to witchcraft, superstition and spiritual darkness. In contrast, I thank God for delivering me from the power of the enemy—I found Christ as my Savior when I was only 10 years old. As a young schoolboy, God began to teach me about the enemy, his tactics and the weapons that are available to us to fight against him.

For more than 30 years now I have dedicated my life to tearing down the strongholds of Satan and building in their place the everlasting kingdom of God. After leaving Africa to attend college in London in the late '70s, I then immigrated to the United States in the early '80s. For more than 20 years now my ministry has been based in the Research Triangle Park area of North Carolina.

Though West Africa is known as an area of great spiritual contrasts (much Christianity and breakthrough as well as a proliferation of witchcraft and voodoo), those contrasts also exist—albeit more subtly—in the United States, western Europe and other "civilized" areas. It is a myth to believe that modern advances, many of which we enjoy in the States, are the keys to good living. On the contrary, it grieves me to see so many good people devastated by Satan's power in our modern world. It grieves me because it is not necessary, since health and healing, prosperity and blessing, salvation and everlasting life are available to us through Jesus Christ, God's Son.

Strangely enough, many people are afraid of God, yet they are not afraid of Satan. Many people do not respect the power of God, while they do respect the power of Satan. Others are afraid to listen to God but are not afraid to listen to Satan. Many people are afraid to obey God but they are willing to obey Satan. If you doubt me, simply turn on your television late at night and tune in to the multitude of infomercials and advertisements for psychics, mediums and tarot card readers. There is a casual, dangerously blasé attitude toward such spiritual practices; people are tapping into Satan, having dismissed God as irrelevant. Or in their well-intentioned search for God, Satan leads them down the wrong path toward "enlightenment"—a path devoid of Christ and true redemption.

This is all due to Satan's terrible ability to deceive. He is a master of deception, and our world is deceived by him. Good has become evil, and evil has become good. Right has become wrong, and wrong has become right.

In the pages of this book, I want to expose the most common and devastating lies that Satan whispers to God's people. Please do not misunderstand me: the purpose is not to fixate on or glorify our enemy but to gain the upper hand in our battle to overcome him. We know the outcome of the war, and we can exult with God in His Word: "They will make war against the Lamb, but the Lamb will overcome them because He is Lord of lords and King of kings— and with him will be his called, chosen and faithful followers" (Rev. 17:14).

Move from a position of one who is defeated, discouraged and overcome by Satan, to one who is victorious in Christ—one of His called, chosen and faithful followers.

My prayer is that the God of Abraham, Isaac and Jacob will use the pages of this book to open your eyes to the truth and deliver you from the snare of the fowler. May you find, through these pages, the freedom you have so desperately been seeking.

Dr. Kingsley Fletcher, Th.D., Ph.D.
Research Triangle Park, North Carolina

PART I

THE ENEMY AND HIS TACTICS

UNDERSTANDING OUR ADVERSARY AND THE BATTLE AGAINST HIM

Be self-controlled and alert. Your enemy the devil prowls around like a roaring lion looking for someone to devour.

1 PETER 5:8

A REAL ENEMY

In my native country of Ghana, there are two seasons: the dry season and the rainy season. Ghana is a steamy, humid nation, where tropical storms bring rain not just in buckets, but in dumpsters! I remember as a child walking home from school one day, getting caught in just such a tropical downpour. One minute I was happy, my book satchel over my shoulder; then literally within 10 seconds, I was completely soaked—that is how hard the rains can fall in Ghana.

In the same way, if we are not walking under God's umbrella of protection, we are vulnerable to the deluge the enemy wants to bring into our lives: storms of sin, depression, financial ruin and chaos.

That is why God has commanded us to put on His armor: to protect us from the attacks of a vicious, ruthless enemy. And rest assured, we are facing a real enemy—we are engaged in a real battle. Some believers already know it, but others still refuse to believe it. Whether you believe it or not doesn't change the truth.

Somebody is plotting your defeat; somebody is tracking you for the kill. This insidious enemy is setting traps for you in the most unexpected places, and he is dedicated to fighting against you every hour of every day. He will not rest until he sees you fall—he is determined to destroy your soul. You must believe it and rise up to take a stand against him.

Most believers today know that something is going wrong in their lives and that some force is working against them. Yet they are afraid or ashamed to admit it and seek help. So they pretend it isn't happening and try to go on normally.

God shows us in His Word that this is not the way to solve the problem. We must face the enemy squarely and push him back—we must stop living in a dream world. We are in a life-and-death struggle, and the enemy of our souls is at work. We are wrestling against "principalities, against powers, against the rulers of the darkness of this world, against spiritual wickedness in high places" (Eph. 6:12, *KJV*). We need God's help.

Our only hope of victory is to "put on" Jesus. Only Jesus, living in us, can protect us from the onslaught of the enemy. If Jesus is in you, Satan will have no point of entry to your life. Jesus becomes your shield of faith—your protective covering when Satan sends his storms. Jesus' presence protects you from the darts being relentlessly hurled at you by the enemy; through Him you are able to "quench" the fiery darts of the wicked one.

God's Word not only points out the existence of the enemy but also describes him in detail and warns us continually to get ready for the battle against him.

This is the same enemy that Jesus had to face:

Then Jesus was led by the Spirit into the desert to be tempted by the devil (Matt. 4:1).

The apostles were also not immune to Satan's attacks:

For we wanted to come to you—certainly I, Paul, did, again and again—but, Satan stopped us (1 Thess. 2:18).

Even the saints of the Old Testament struggled constantly with the adversary:

Then he showed me Joshua the high priest standing before the angel of the LORD, and Satan standing at his right side to accuse him (Zech. 3:1).

This is not a game; this is serious business. You must wake up. You must be vigilant. Something is happening that will determine your future and the future of your family. That something is Satan's plan to destroy your life by bringing sin, addiction, depression, sickness, calamity—anything to make you believe that you are no longer a victor in Christ. By simply making you *believe* the lie of disqualification, even if it is not true, hasn't Satan achieved his goal of making you ineffective for God's kingdom?

Why is Satan so angry, and why is he running after you and me? Why does he want to destroy us? Why does he have no mercy—even on innocent little babies? Think about it: Babies don't deserve to suffer and die. They don't deserve sickness or pain. But Satan doesn't care about that. He hates God's creation and is determined to destroy us all. As well, he is very jealous of you. "Why," you might ask, "would Satan be jealous of me?" Because you, and all humans, are the only beings who have the ability to procreate in God's image. Satan was not made in God's image; neither does he have the ability to beget life. And that angers him—greatly. So his goal is to destroy life.

Satan is bitter because he once had a place in the heart of God. Before the earth was formed, before the creation of humankind, God had angels, heavenly spirit beings, that surrounded Him. Their major responsibility was to give Him praise and glory. God set Lucifer to be the head of them, and Lucifer was a glorious being.

His beauty and his glory resulted in his downfall, for pride entered into his heart (see Isa. 14:11-15).

Lucifer saw his worth and knew his abilities. He gloried in his beauty and wallowed in his charm. He believed that his wisdom excelled all others. And he said to himself, *Now that God has made me an executive and has given me authority, I think I will turn the tables on Him. Yes, I will topple God! Then everyone will recognize my greatness!*

God has never been able to tolerate pride. Because of that, Satan was cast out of heaven and, since the day he fell, has been plotting to get back at God. He hates God with a passion and he hates God's Word. He hates God's Church; he hates God's people. He believes that he has hit on the perfect way to hurt God and get back at Him.

What could be worse for a father than to see his children suffer? What could be worse than to see a child go astray and ruin his or her life? What could be worse than alienation from a child? These are the thoughts that play on Satan's mind. His delight is to turn God's children away from Him, to cause them to suffer, to lead them into disobedience and alienation from

> Satan knows that he can never defeat God. That's why he picks on us.

the Father. Satan's highest goal is to destroy God's children total-ly—body and soul. When he is successful, his cackle of glee rings out through the darkened passages of hell.

Satan knows that he can never defeat God. That's why he picks on us. He knows he will never win in a direct confrontation with the Father, so he goes after the children.

Satan will use any tactic, try any trick. Nothing is too vile for him. Nothing is too ugly. Nothing is too filthy. He has no pity. He is ruthless and utterly cruel.

Satan knows how God has prepared blessings for each one of us. He knows that we are destined for greatness and that we are born to be free. That's why he never stops harassing us and is deter-mined to keep us enslaved. He wants to make us his own children:

> The field is the world, and the good seed stands for the sons of the kingdom. The weeds are the sons of the evil one, and the enemy who sows them is the devil (Matt. 13:38).

> This is how we know who the children of God are and who the children of the devil are: Anyone who does not do what is right is not a child of God; nor is anyone who does not love his brother (1 John 3:10).

Satan is determined to turn back believers. Many who have received the Lord as their personal Savior are later heard to say: "I don't know what is happening to me. It looks like I cannot contin-ue in the faith. I want to serve God, but something is pulling me away from the service of the Lord. One part of me wants to go to church, while another part of me wants to sin. I want to live right, and I don't understand why I am drawn to do these other things."

When we understand the tactics of a real enemy, it is easy to see why Christians are going through these struggles. Satan knows God's purpose in the life of the believer. Since he doesn't like God, we become his targets too. Since his downfall, he has been aware of God's great plans for us. He is jealous of us because we have the blessings of God in our lives. He will do anything and everything to spoil your future. Anything! Everything!

We are not dealing with a fool. Satan has been around for a long time and was created with higher intelligence. When he fell, God took his power from him, but He did not take all of his ability from him—he still has much of it.

Satan is not fooling around because he knows that his time is short. He knows his ultimate end. Hell was not prepared for people but for Satan and his rebellious troops. It is a place reserved for rebels. Satan knows this and is determined not to go there alone. He is determined to drag down with him as many of God's children as he can. That's why he is chasing you.

You must wake up to this fact—you must be *on guard*. Be sober! Be vigilant! We face a real enemy.

Pray for Truth

Dear Father, I know that if I walk away from You, I will walk out from under the protection of Your love and care and make myself vulnerable to the attacks of the enemy. Please help me to stay close to You through Your Son, and help me to be aware of the battle raging around me. Father, I want to be victorious in You, I want to do great things for You, and I want my family to experience Your blessings. Help me, Lord, to walk a straight path, aware of the snares of Satan, victorious through the blood of Christ. Amen.

CHAPTER 2

*Lest Satan should take advantage of us; for we are not
ignorant of his devices.*

2 CORINTHIANS 2:11, *NKJV*

THE TACTICS
SATAN EMPLOYS

Our greatest defense is to know our enemy and to understand his
purposes and the tactics he employs to bring them about. If we are
ignorant of the devices of Satan, he can take advantage of us.
However, if we are not ignorant of his devices, he is powerless to
harm us. It is that simple.

None of us likes to be taken advantage of, yet sometimes it
happens. People who don't know how to read and write, for example, are often taken advantage of. Some of them don't know their
rights. Others are afraid to claim their rights, for some reason.

Here is another example: A newly arrived immigrant is entitled
to receive legal minimum wage for his labor. Because he hasn't yet
learned the value of the dollar, his boss pays him only four dollars
an hour. In his ignorance, he is happy with that because he doesn't

know any better. Unless someone informs him that he is entitled to much more, he doesn't know to claim his rightful wage. For the time being, someone is taking advantage of him.

That is exactly what Satan is doing to many people—even to many believers. He may be doing it to you; he may be robbing you blind. You may be entitled to much more than you are receiving. If so, you must first discover his tricks. Then you must stand up and demand your rights. You must put the thief in his place. If you learn his tactics, Satan will have difficulty taking advantage of you.

Satan fears an informed believer and runs the other way when he sees one. He dreads those who have put on their spiritual armor. Satan is a coward, and he cowers in fear in the presence of the shield of faith (see Eph. 6:16). He knows that his darts are powerless against that shield.

Ignorance is *not* bliss. Ignorance is tragedy. Ignorance of God's will is the greatest tragedy in life. We must become *informed* about the important issues of life. If we don't, Satan will cheat us every day.

When I was a boy, I loved to trap mice. My father taught me how to do it. I could hear those mice running through our house, especially when the lights were out. If we didn't catch them, they would eat all the unrefrigerated vegetables we had stored for the family. So before I went to bed, I would set my trap. In the middle of the night, I would hear the trap click and the mouse squeak, and I would exult, "I've got him!" Sure enough, the next morning I would find a dead mouse in the trap.

I can picture the devil's trap. He has put the finest cheese in it. It is so beautiful! Sometimes he uses the finest fish or the best meat. It is so well placed! He knows what he is doing because he is a practiced hunter.

A mouse walks by and sees the trap. He senses that the trap doesn't belong there and is set up to hurt him. He thinks, *I'm not about to be trapped in there. I'm too clever for that,* and he begins to walk away.

Ignorance

is *not* bliss.

Ignorance

is tragedy.

Ignorance of

God's will is

the greatest

tragedy in

life.

After a few steps, the mouse turns back to see if the cheese is still there. Sure enough, it hasn't moved. *I know this is a trick,* he thinks. *He won't get me, that's for sure.*

He turns again to go, but he catches the smell of it. How alluring! Cheddar, his favorite type of cheese! How did they know? *I won't be tricked,* he thinks, *but it can't hurt anything to stay here for a moment smelling it, can it?*

He waits for a few moments and nothing happens. No one is watching. He decides to go closer to inspect it. It still looks like a trap to him, but his desire for the taste of it begins to make him believe that he might outfox the hunter, take the bait and leave unscathed.

He slowly approaches the bait again. After an agonizing moment of hesitation, he decides that it couldn't hurt to take a little nibble. *I won't go too far. Just a little! Then, I'll run out of here safely and leave the trap standing empty.*

With the first nibble, he is astonished. He never imagined that any cheese could taste so good. It is delightful! He continues to take small bites around the edges, careful not to set off the dreaded trap. But as he savors each delicious morsel, his mind strays more and more from the danger. *How could anything that tastes so good be bad?* Maybe he has been wrong to be so cautious. *This is wonderful!*

The next day he approaches the trap again, and lo and behold, there sits a fresh bit of cheese! He steps back a bit as he savors the delicacy, and he sees anew the terrible jaws of the trap. But mysteriously, the jaws no longer appear as menacing as before. He begins to grow accustomed to them. He has gone far enough now, with no apparent repercussions, that he begins to feel confident that no harm will come to him. He will not be trapped. He will enjoy his meal and go on his way, as before.

I'm very clever, he thinks. *I know how to get what I want without suffering any consequences.* And in this state of self-delusion he works his way into the very center of the trap. With quiet confidence he thrusts his snout into the juicy tidbit. Then, without warning, the terrible jaws snap shut.

Crack!

He cries out for help. When no one seems to hear, he screams. He is in agony. Why can't anyone hear him? He screams louder but to no avail.

Satan's snare is so attractive, and playing with it doesn't seem to hurt today. But believe me, if it doesn't get you today it will get you tomorrow.

This trap is not just for "bad" people. Satan loves to catch "good" people in his trap. He loves to catch young people, innocent people, religious people, Baptists, Pentecostals, Methodists—in this regard, he is no respecter of persons.

How can good people possibly be trapped in this way? It is because Satan presents such an ingenious deception. It is because he is a master deceiver, a most clever enemy. And it is only in mastering his own tactics that we can effectively defeat him.

Now that you are aware of the seriousness of this threat, I want to show you in the following pages exactly how Satan thinks and acts. I want to make you aware of his tactics as never before.

Open your heart to God and let Him speak to you as you read this book.

Pray for Truth

Dear God, I want to be armed and prepared to withstand the attacks of the wicked one in my life. Help me, Father, to be informed and aware of the tactics the enemy wants to employ against me. Lord, just thinking about this subject makes me uncomfortable—a bit fearful. I pray that You would take away my fear as I take refuge in You. Help me, dear God, to be open to the leading of the Holy Spirit, aware of the tactics of Satan and prepared to respond as You lead me in my life. In the name of Jesus I pray. Amen.

PART II

LIES SATAN WANTS YOU TO BELIEVE

COMBATTING 14 COMMON
LIES THE ENEMY USES TO
TRY TO TEAR DOWN
BELIEVERS AND THE CHURCH

CHAPTER 3

Satan himself masquerades as an angel of light.

2 CORINTHIANS 11:14

LIE:

"SATAN DOESN'T EVEN EXIST"

An old southern preacher was in the pulpit one Sunday, preaching fire and brimstone to his mesmerized congregation. Way in the back, arms folded tight against his chest, sat old Mr. Johnson. In this small rural community, Mr. Johnson was known as the resident atheist. Every now and then, he would slip into the back pew just to heckle the preacher.

Toward the end of the sermon, just when the preacher was reaching his crescendo, old Mr. Johnson stood up and yelled, "Oh yeah? Well, I don't believe in hell. Nor do I believe in God or the devil."

"Well," said the preacher, taking Mr. Johnson's interruption in stride, "the devil believes in you, John, and so does God."

With that, Mr. Johnson sat down—for the moment.

The preacher continued preaching about those who are not saved and how they will be cast into hell. Picking up his big, black Bible, he opened to Luke 13:28 and read: "There will be weeping there, and gnashing of teeth, when you see Abraham, Isaac and Jacob and all the prophets in the kingdom of God, but yourselves thrown out."

Mr. Johnson rose again, proudly, and said, "Look here!"

Slowly, reluctantly, the congregation turned around to look at Mr. Johnson, who had proceeded to remove his false teeth. With a gleam in his eye, he said, "No teeth! How can there be gnashing of teeth if I don't have any teeth?!"

A few in the small church smiled and chuckled under their breath as all eyes turned back to the old, wise preacher, who calmly laid down his Bible, regarded Mr. Johnson with a sympathetic look, and said, "Oh, have no worry, Mr. Johnson, teeth will be provided."

Like old man Johnson, many people today say boldly, "I don't believe in the devil." If you are one of those people, I want to tell you that it doesn't matter what you believe or don't believe: Satan is real and he is out to get you.

Our problem today is that we are so well educated and we know so much. We are trained to depend upon our reasoning, and we have developed our minds to reason out life's problems. Because the existence of Satan cannot be scientifically proven and isn't logical, many no longer believe that he exists.

I once heard a wise preacher say, "If you don't believe there is a devil, try to live one day for God. You will find out quickly that your enemy exists." He was right. Satan hates those who try to live for God. If he is not bothering you, it might be because he thinks he already has you in his control.

If you do not believe in a personal devil, you are deceived. This deception is not limited to young people being raised in our twenty-first-century, post-Christian culture. Older people are also doubting or denying the existence of Satan. As a matter of fact, a recent study showed that 47 percent of *born-again Christians* do not believe that Satan is a living being but is merely a symbol of evil. (It begs the question, What Bible are they reading?) For those who are not born again, the number who do not believe in the devil rises to 65 percent.[1] Yet the existence of Satan is one of the most well-documented facts of Scripture:

> How you have fallen from heaven, O morning star, son of the dawn! You have been cast down to the earth, you who once laid low the nations! You said in your heart, "I will ascend to heaven; I will raise my throne above the stars of God; I will sit enthroned on the mount of assembly, on the utmost heights of the sacred mountain. I will ascend above the tops of the clouds; I will make myself like the Most High" (Isa. 14:12-14).

> You were the model of perfection, full of wisdom and perfect in beauty. You were in Eden, the garden of God; every precious stone adorned you: ruby, topaz and emerald, chrysolite, onyx and jasper, sapphire, turquoise and beryl. Your settings and mountings were made of gold; on the day you were created they were prepared. You were anointed as a guardian cherub, for so I ordained you. You were on the holy mount of God; you walked among the fiery stones. You were blameless in your ways from the day you were created till wickedness was found in you. Through your widespread trade you were filled with violence, and you sinned. So I drove you in disgrace from the mount of God, and I expelled you, O guardian cherub, from among the fiery stones. Your heart became proud on account of your beauty, and you corrupted your wisdom because of your splendor. So I threw you to the earth; I made a spectacle of you before kings (Ezek. 28:12-17).

The Bible uses many names to describe Satan. Most of them show us his character. He is the accuser:

> Then I heard a loud voice in heaven say: "Now have come the salvation and the power and the kingdom of our God, and the authority of his Christ. For the accuser of our brothers, who accuses them before our God day and night, has been hurled down" (Rev. 12:10).

He is the adversary:

> Be self-controlled and alert. Your enemy the devil prowls around like a roaring lion looking for someone to devour (1 Pet. 5:8).

He is the wicked one:

> When anyone hears the message about the kingdom and does not understand it, the evil one comes and snatches away what was sown in his heart (Matt. 13:19).

He is the tempter:

> The tempter came to him and said, "If you are the Son of God, tell these stones to become bread" (Matt. 4:3).

He is the god of this world:

> The god of this age has blinded the minds of unbelievers, so that they cannot see the light of the gospel of the glory of Christ, who is the image of God (2 Cor. 4:4).

He is the ruler of the kingdom of the air:

You may reach a positive conclusion from what Satan has told you, but your conclusion is a deception.

As for you, you were dead in your transgressions and sins, in which you used to live when you followed the ways of this world and of the ruler of the kingdom of the air, the spirit who is now at work in those who are disobedient (Eph. 2:1-2).

He is a murderer. But, above all, he is a liar:

You belong to your father, the devil, and you want to carry out your father's desire. He was a murderer from the beginning, not holding to the truth, for there is no truth in him. When he lies, he speaks his native language, for he is a liar and the father of lies (John 8:44).

Satan is a confirmed liar. He never tells the truth about himself. A murderer doesn't tell the truth. A thief doesn't tell the truth. How can we expect Satan to tell the truth? He is the father of lies.

Yet, he never identifies himself as the tempter. He never calls himself a deceiver. He doesn't want us to know that he is the evil one.

Satan never tells the whole truth, but he may tell you a half-truth. When part of what he says is correct, you may accept the rest of his line—but you can be sure that most of it will turn out to be lies. And when he does use part truths, it is only to deceive and bring about evil, never good. You may reach a positive conclusion from what Satan has told you, but your conclusion is a deception. You may sincerely believe that you are right, but you may be sincerely wrong.

It was Satan's lies to Adam and Eve that caused their downfall. He cleverly convinced them to disobey God. Interestingly, they were not unintelligent people; they were created in the image of God and walked and talked with God. Regarding the fruit from the tree of the knowledge of good and evil, they were deceived because Satan's lie to them was very clever. The Scriptures tell it like this:

"You will not surely die," the serpent said to the woman. "For God knows that when you eat of it your eyes will be opened, and you will be like God, knowing good and evil." When the woman saw that the fruit of the tree was good for food and pleasing to the eye, and also desirable for gaining wisdom, she took some and ate it. She also gave some to her husband, who was with her, and he ate it (Gen. 3:4-6).

What a master deceiver Satan is! He can make people believe anything. He even convinces people that he doesn't exist.

If I were Satan, I would never appear as a devil or an evil being. I would disguise myself as a friend or someone who is truly concerned with people's problems. I would appear as an angel of light. And that is exactly what he does.

Pray for Truth

Precious Father, You are the Father of lights, and in You there is no shifting shadow. Help me today, Lord, to walk soberly in the knowledge that we wrestle not against flesh and blood. But though

*my enemy is real and is a master deceiver, I know that in You
there is all truth. Help me also to understand that with Christ as
my protector, I do not need to cower in the presence of the enemy.
Be my shield, O God, and help me to be an instrument of
Your saving truth in the lives of those perishing in Satan's
deceptions. Amen.*

Note

1. George Barna, *Boiling Point* (Ventura: Regal Books, 2001), p. 193.

For he is the kind of man who is always thinking about the cost.

P R O V E R B S   2 3 : 7

LIE:

"YOU CAN ALWAYS TRUST YOUR FEELINGS AND THOUGHTS"

What child do you know who when asked what he or she wants to be when grown up, says, "an alcoholic"? No one sets out to be an addict, but there are many addicts these days. Many people become alcoholics because they are deceived. It may be true that some people are more genetically inclined to become an alcoholic than others, but this does not automatically mean they will. Ultimately, Satan gets control of their feelings and of their thought life.

To keep people from hearing the Father's voice of love, Satan never ceases to repeat his lies to those whom he has trapped.

So many people get hooked on drugs. They think, *I can stop when I want to.* They are deceived. Once they are hooked and are no longer free to make their own decisions, they begin to sell everything they own and, when that is all gone, to steal anything they can lay their hands on to satisfy their craving. Their thought life comes under Satan's control, slowly but surely—until it's too late.

Good women are having abortions. They are deceived into thinking they are doing the correct thing. They are convinced that this is not only their "right" but that it *is right.* Now if you, reader, have had an abortion, you need to know that there is forgiveness waiting for you in Jesus' arms. All you need to do is ask.

I am not trying to condemn anyone but simply to show that well-intentioned people are being duped and deceived—via their thoughts and emotions—to do things that are contrary to God's will.

This type of deception doesn't happen overnight. Little by little Satan gains control of people's emotions and thoughts, until he has them under his power. Most people don't even know what is happening to them.

If I were Satan, I would work on your feelings. I would work on the way you think. I would know what you want, and I would give you what you want, until I had you in my power. This is Satan's ultimate goal.

When most people are caught in their crime or vice, they invariably say "It wasn't my fault," or "I couldn't help myself."

What ingenious deceit! Satan knows that if he controls the thought life, he controls the person. This is entering into the realm of strongholds of the mind. We must recognize strongholds for what they are: illusions and machinations of Satan that he uses to keep us enslaved to his lies. The words of 2 Corinthians 10 hone in on this battle for our minds:

> The weapons we fight with are not the weapons of the world. On the contrary, they have divine power to demolish strongholds. We demolish *arguments* and every *pretension* that sets itself up against the *knowledge* of God, and we take captive every *thought* to make it obedient to Christ (2 Cor. 10:4-5, emphasis mine).

Notice the mind-related words: "arguments," "pretension," "knowledge," "thought." Satan will constantly attack you through your thoughts and emotions: Prepare yourself for the battle by taking every thought captive to make it obedient to God's purposes, not Satan's.

He tells people that once they are bound, there is no way for them to be freed (thus, a stronghold). He tells them that there is no escape, no way out. He makes them feel hopeless and helpless. He makes them believe that God doesn't love them anymore and that they have done things so terrible that they can never be forgiven.

All the while, the Father stands with His arms extended, calling to His errant children: "Here I am! I stand at the door and knock. If anyone hears my voice and opens the door, I will come in and eat with him, and he with me" (Rev. 3:20). He is saying: "And everyone who calls on the name of the Lord will be saved" (Acts 2:21). He is the loving Father who welcomes home the prodigal son with rejoicing:

> The son said to him, "Father, I have sinned against heaven and against you. I am no longer worthy to be called your son." But the father said to his servants, "Quick! Bring the best robe and put it on him. Put a ring on his finger and sandals on his feet. Bring the fattened calf and kill it. Let's have a feast and celebrate. For this son of mine was dead and is alive again; he was lost and is found." So they began to celebrate (Luke 15:21-24).

To keep people from hearing the Father's voice of love, Satan never ceases to repeat his lies to those he has trapped. "There is no escape from the downward pull of doom. There is no way out," he says. He even puts the blame on God and makes people angry, believing that God acts in His own interests and that He has forgotten them and forsaken them. "When God acts," he tells them, "it is in favor of a select group."

In this way, Satan makes people bitter toward God and their fellow humankind. He is the master deceiver, with centuries of experience to hone his trade.

Pray for Truth

Dear God, I give myself to You once again so that You will be in control of my thoughts and emotions. I know that if I surrender my emotions to You, Lord, that You will guide me in my responses and reactions to everyday life. Father, please guard my heart and my mind, and allow me to be sober-minded, aware of the attacks of the enemy on my thought life and emotional life. Dear Lord, right now I surrender every thought captive to You. I ask You to purify my mind and emotions and guide me in my decisions today. In Christ's precious name. Amen.

By faith Moses, when he was come to years, refused to be called the son of Pharaoh's daughter; choosing rather to suffer affliction with the people of God, than to enjoy the pleasures of sin for a season.

HEBREWS 11:24-25, KJV

LIE:

"SIN IS ACCEPTABLE AND CARRIES FEW CONSEQUENCES"

In the modern arena of high-concept marketing campaigns, one advertiser outdoes the rest: Satan. Look closely and you will see the enemy's complete public relations campaign, which goes to great lengths to convince people that sin is beautiful, harmless and great—that sin brings happiness and bears no consequences. If I were Satan, I would make sin so lovely that I would cause the eyes of people to lust after evil. They would be ready to pay any price for it.

I would never let them know that sin is disobeying the Word of God. I would gloss over the fact that sin is displeasing to God, breaks the Father's heart and demands that He respond with correction. I would cause them to forget the words of sacred Scripture:

> For every living soul belongs to me, the father as well as the son—both alike belong to me. The soul who sins is the one who will die (Ezek. 18:4).

> For the wages of sin is death, but the gift of God is eternal life in Christ Jesus our Lord (Rom. 6:23).

If I were Satan, I would actually take the word "sin" out of some dictionaries and replace it with more positive and lovely words. In everyday conversation, I would change the word "adultery" to "meaningful relationship." I would change "homosexual lifestyle" to "alternate lifestyle." I would change "fornication" to "premarital sex." I would make sin so attractive that people would like it.

This is exactly what Satan is doing. Then, when he has deceived people and convinced them to yield to him, he stands behind them and roars with laughter: "Ha! I knew I would get you. It was only a matter of time. I am a genius."

Have you ever been approached by someone selling fake Rolex watches? In fact, they actually do look like Rolexes, but they don't cost thousands of dollars (as does a real Rolex). They are much cheaper because they are fakes. Many people buy these fake watches because they are so beautiful. Satan is like the champion fake-Rolex salesman. He is selling his line successfully to millions of otherwise intelligent people.

We need to take a stand against this deceit. Unless we say no to the devil and to sin, he will reign over our homes and families. He will reign over our churches. When we say yes to sin, we lose control of our lives and hand authority to Satan.

Sin has become so attractive today that we find it in every neighborhood. Neighbors are fighting each other, and violence becomes a reality as tempers flare. Some of the perpetrators then turn around Sunday morning and act very holy as they walk into church.

Sin has become so attractive today that we are finding it more and more in the Church. We have pews filled with hypocrites who refuse to hear the Word of God or receive Christ as their Savior, refuse to shake hands with one another and refuse to let God change their lives. Where is the outward evidence—the deeds— of their so-called faith (see Jas. 2:26)? "If I die, don't come to my funeral," they say. "I am going home to be with God." I would like to ask these people a question: "Which home are you going to?" They certainly aren't going to God's home. No sin will enter there.

> But the cowardly, the unbe-
> lieving, the vile, the murder-
> ers, the sexually immoral,
> those who practice magic
> arts, the idolaters and all
> liars—their place will be in
> the fiery lake of burning sul-
> fur. This is the second death
> (Rev. 21:8).

Sin has infected our families— our brothers and sisters, our children.

If we want to see the glory and peace of God return to our families, we must take a stand against the enemy who is devastating our loved ones.

If we want to see the glory and peace of God return to our families, we must take a stand against the enemy who is devastating our loved ones. How? By rebuking the devil in our homes; by putting on the armor of God every day and inviting the Holy Spirit to do a complete spiritual housecleaning in our lives and the lives of our families; by confessing our sins one to another and extending forgiveness and releasing bitterness.

Believers have compromised so much with sin that when the Word of God is preached and begins to prick their hearts, their response is "No! Not yet!" Some find sin so attractive that they respond with anger and leave their churches, vowing never to return.

When God deals with us about sin, it is because He wants to set us free. At such moments the devil tells us to get up and leave the church, never to go back. He doesn't want us to receive God's Word into our hearts; he wants to see us destroyed. But we cannot live without the Word of God. Satan's way is not satisfying—he has come only to steal, kill and destroy. We need God's blessing; His ways are life. Satan only offers death: "The thief comes only to steal and kill and destroy; I have come that they may have life, and have it to the full" (John 10:10).

When God begins to work in your heart, the devil will start making you uncomfortable. He will become scared. He doesn't want the Holy Spirit talking to you. Why? Because he doesn't want you to hear the truth. He wants you to be offended and storm off. Then, he'll win. But God's Word is true: "Do not be deceived: God cannot be mocked. A man reaps what he sows" (Gal. 6:7).

Recognize sin for what it is. Don't break the Father's heart by playing around with the enemy. Get on God's side and receive victory over sin and the devil.

Pray for Truth
Dear God, it is sometimes difficult for me to resist sin in my life. But just as bad, I find myself not wanting to admit my sins to You

or to another believer. Lord, help me walk in Your grace, mercy and truth, acknowledging sin when it comes into my life and confessing it to You promptly. And, Lord, for those areas that have become strongholds or addictions, help me to find the courage to also confide in another believer, seeking accountability and discipline. Help me, precious Father, to surrender my sins, and my attitudes about sin, to You every day. In Jesus' name. Amen.

Then he told them many things in parables, saying: "A farmer went out to sow his seed. As he was scattering the seed, some fell along the path, and the birds came and ate it up. Some fell on rocky places, where it did not have much soil. It sprang up quickly, because the soil was shallow. But when the sun came up, the plants were scorched, and they withered because they had no root. Other seed fell among thorns, which grew up and choked the plants. Still other seed fell on good soil, where it produced a crop— a hundred, sixty or thirty times what was sown. He who has ears, let him hear."

M A T T H E W   1 3 : 3 - 9

LIE:
"THE WORD OF GOD IS NOT ALWAYS EFFECTIVE"

Satan will do everything he can to hinder the Word of God from becoming a real, tangible, active part of your life. Many believers still do not understand: "The word of God is living and active. Sharper than any double-edged sword, it penetrates even to dividing soul and spirit, joints and marrow; it judges the thoughts and attitudes of the heart" (Heb. 4:12).

Satan knows that in order for him to defeat God's plans for His people, the Word must be hindered. If the Word is allowed to sink into the hearts of people, it will bring deliverance to them—deliverance from sin, sickness, infirmity and pain. The very thought is frightening to our enemy. The Word has power to destroy the devil's entire kingdom. He is determined that it not be given free course.

Just as in the parable of the sower, I could think of a number of ways to hinder the effect of the Word, if I were Satan.

If I were Satan, I would tell sinners that the Bible is so holy that they dare not touch it until they get right with God. That is a lie. That's like saying you should not go see your doctor until you have recovered from your pneumonia—it makes no sense! If you begin to open the Bible, you will begin to get right with God. Don't let the sin in your life hinder you from searching God's Word. If you read the Bible, you will learn how to overcome sin. The Bible will teach you how to live right.

If I were Satan, I would tell people that the Bible is so holy, they should show respect for it by putting it under their pillow at night as protection from demons. Mind you, they should never actually *open* their Bible, but just kind of have it around as a good luck charm. Then before they sleep, they can say: "Now I lay me down to sleep, I pray the Lord my soul to keep."

Many people are not taking the Word of God any more seriously than that. But God didn't intend for His Word to be hidden under your pillow. He intended for it to take up residence in your heart.

Some believers haven't used their Bible for so long that they don't even know where it is. It is on some shelf collecting dust or packed away in some dusty box—somewhere. Satan loves that. He doesn't want you to put on the whole armor of God. He wants you to be weak against his advances.

If I were Satan, I would convince people to limit their study of the Bible to Sunday morning church services. There was a time in the Church of England (which later became the Anglican Church) when the Bible was chained to the pulpit. It was so costly and so

Nearly 60 percent of all American adults do not typically read a Bible in any given week.

scarce that anyone who wanted to read it had to come to the church. It could not be taken out.

Although the Bible is now readily available to most believers (thanks to Gutenberg and his printing press), that same thing is happening today. The devil is tying the Word of God to the church. He is making people believe that they should concentrate on the Word of God only when they are in the church building. The Word is not going out with people. It is not going into their hearts. Many believers never open the Bible during the week. They are deceived and robbed of its benefits.

According to George Barna, in 1990 about 45 percent of all adults said they read the Bible during a typical week. By 2000, that number had dropped to 40 percent, and Barna projects that by 2010, the number will be somewhere around 32 percent (a depressing statistic!).[1] That means that nearly three-fifths, or 60 percent, of all American adults do not typically read a Bible in any given week.

If I were Satan, I would get very busy when God begins to minister to people's hearts in the service. I would tell them that the message was for someone else—the person beside them, or someone who didn't even attend church that day; anyone else—but not for them personally.

I would try to make people forget the message even before they get out the door. I would change their thoughts to other things. I would remind them of bills to be paid, jobs to be done, problems to be solved or of good food waiting to be eaten.

I would use other people to spread gossip right in the aisles of the church and change the subject to scandalous things that happen in the community—anything to cause them to forget the Word. I would cause them to be like the rocks upon which the seed can't find root. I would cause them to be like a trodden path, too hardened to give place to the seed.

Why would Satan go to all this trouble over an old book? I want to tell you: That "old book" has power. It is the living Word of God, divinely inspired: "All Scripture is God-breathed and is useful for teaching, rebuking, correcting and training in righteousness" (2 Tim. 3:16).

That divinely inspired Word has power to keep you from sin:

I have hidden your word in my heart that I might not sin against you (Ps. 119:11).

That God-breathed Word has power to heal your sick body:

He sent forth his word and healed them; he rescued them from the grave (Ps. 107:20).

If you are a sinner, that Word will help you to be born again and become a child of God:

For you have been born again, not of perishable seed, but of imperishable, through the living and enduring word of God (1 Pet. 1:23).

That Word has power to help you overcome the wicked one:

> I write to you, fathers, because you have known him who is from the beginning. I write to you, young men, because you are strong, and the word of God lives in you, and you have overcome the evil one (1 John 2:14).

No wonder Satan hates the Word of God!

If I were Satan, I would tell people not to pay too much attention to the preacher. After all, they know the Word for themselves. They don't need anyone else to interpret it for them. If people know the Word so well, why don't they live by the Word?

If I were Satan, I would cause religious people to go to church only on special occasions—Christmas, New Year's Eve, Easter, Mother's Day, Father's Day and wedding or funeral services.

Satan is happy when we restrict church attendance to these special occasions. It works in his favor.

If I were Satan, I would do exactly what he is doing.

Pray for Truth

Dear God, help me to never take Your Word for granted and always to be a student of the Bible. Forgive me, Lord, for not appreciating Your Word as much as I should, and help me to read and study it diligently. But more importantly, Father, allow Your Holy Spirit to guide me in my study of the Scriptures, allowing me to feast upon the wonderful truths and treasures found within. And help me, Lord, to appreciate the teaching of the Word in my church, as you speak through my pastor.
In Jesus' name I pray. Amen.

Note

1. George Barna, *Boiling Point* (Ventura: Regal Books, 2001), p. 213.

CHAPTER 7

*But you will receive power when the Holy Spirit comes on you;
and you will be my witnesses in Jerusalem, and in all Judea and
Samaria, and to the ends of the earth.*

ACTS 1:8

LIE:
"THE HOLY SPIRIT IS NOT ACTIVE TODAY"

Satan certainly does not want you to believe in the Holy Spirit and all the supernatural manifestations that accompany the Holy Spirit.

If I were Satan, I would say, "Speaking in tongues? That's crazy! Come on! We're living in the twenty-first century. Don't talk to me about that Dark Ages stuff."

I would convince people that speaking in tongues passed away with the death of the first-century apostles.

I would tell people how important it is to stand on their religious traditions and ignore anything in the Bible that isn't included in their denominational history.

Peter and John were not intimidated by the power of Satan to cripple and destroy. They didn't have Ph.D.s, but they had the Holy Spirit.

The devil doesn't want believers to have power. He doesn't want them to be witnesses. He doesn't want the gospel to be preached in the whole world. He doesn't want believers to pray in the Spirit, walk in the Spirit and live in the Spirit.

If I were Satan, I would tell people, "Don't believe that teaching about speaking in tongues. That is dangerous. Anyone who speaks in tongues has a mental problem. That person is probably under demonic influence."

I would cause believers to ignore what the Bible says about speaking in tongues: "For if I pray in a tongue, my spirit prays" (1 Cor. 14:14).

The devil doesn't want me to know that "my spirit prays" when I am praying in tongues. He is afraid that we will become too spiritual and will walk in the power of God. He will do anything to see that we continue to walk in the flesh.

If I were Satan, I would convince ministers to forbid the speaking of tongues in church, ignoring what the Bible says: "Therefore, my brothers, be eager to prophesy, and do not forbid speaking in tongues" (1 Cor. 14:39).

Why does the Bible warn us not to forbid the practice of speaking in tongues? Because great power is released when we speak in the Spirit. So much power, in fact, that Satan gets scared. He doesn't want you to be speaking a heavenly language that he can't understand! He doesn't want you to know and understand the things of God.

Before I received the gift of tongues, I was scared of the devil. Anytime I saw something that resembled his work, I ran away. But since I received the gift of tongues through the Holy Spirit, he is now scared of me. When I get on my knees and open my mouth to pray, he says: "Look out! Here comes that man of God. Here comes that one who will not compromise with me. He is coming to lash at me again."

I have learned the secrets of overcoming Satan: I obey the Bible and I submit myself to God through the Spirit. Then when I resist Satan, he runs away from me. God said: "Submit yourselves, then, to God. Resist the devil, and he will flee from you" (Jas. 4:7).

Praise God! I love His Word. It gives me power over the wicked one. I refuse to listen to the enemy's lies against the Holy Spirit. It was the power of the Holy Spirit that made the disciples successful. When Jesus was taken from the earth and had gone to present Himself and to take His place with the Father, the disciples were left alone.

They were very common people, but they had the privilege of being with Jesus for more than three years. They had seen Him change the lives of sinners. They had seen Him make the crippled walk. They had even seen Him raise the dead.

Jesus had promised them that He would never forsake them. Now He had returned physically to heaven, and they were alone. But Jesus was true to His Word. He sent them the Comforter. Through the Holy Spirit, He was with them to confirm the Word they preached everywhere in His name.

And it worked. Peter and John, who were uneducated fishermen, were going to the Temple to pray when they met a crippled man begging for money. I love what Peter told him: "Silver or gold I do not have, but what I have I give you. In the name of Jesus Christ of Nazareth, walk" (Acts 3:6).

These men were not intimidated by the power of Satan to cripple and destroy. They had Jesus living in them. He was in their hearts and on their lips. He was their shield of faith. "Taking him by the right hand, he helped him up, and instantly the man's feet and ankles became strong" (Acts 3:7).

Who told Peter what to do to help the man be delivered? He didn't have a Ph.D., but he had the Holy Spirit. The Holy Spirit will give you wisdom and show you exactly what to do in any given situation. If the Holy Spirit is working in you, something supernatural will happen when you call upon the name of Jesus.

The reason most Christians are being constantly battered by the enemy is that they are afraid of the Holy Spirit. Many believers run away from Him. The way He does things is strange to them. When He begins to move, they begin to get nervous because they don't know what is happening. They don't realize that the Holy Spirit is the Energizer.

You can't stand still or keep quiet when the Energizer starts moving. The Holy Spirit is our Energizer: Let Him energize you.

When the work of the first-century Church grew and more workers were needed, the apostles instructed the people to search for those with special qualifications:

> "Brothers, choose seven men from among you who are known to be full of the Spirit and wisdom. We will turn this responsibility over to them and will give our attention to prayer and the ministry of the word." This proposal pleased the whole group. They chose Stephen, a man full of faith and of the Holy Spirit; also Philip, Procorus, Nicanor, Timon, Parmenas, and Nicolas from Antioch, a convert to Judaism (Acts 6:3-5).

One of the seven men chosen was Stephen. He became a giant of faith and was the first Christian martyr. He was a "man full of faith and of the Holy Spirit."

The Holy Spirit can make you a giant of faith. With the power of the Holy Spirit, you can overcome the enemy. Because the power of the Holy Spirit was in Stephen, he did great wonders: "Now Stephen, a man full of God's grace and power, did great wonders and miraculous signs among the people" (Acts 6:8).

If God could make Stephen an overcomer, He can make you an overcomer too. If Stephen could do great wonders and miracles, you can do great wonders and miracles also—through the power of the Holy Spirit.

When the disciples had chosen these men and had placed them in positions of responsibility, something wonderful happened in Jerusalem: "So the word of God spread. The number of disciples in Jerusalem increased rapidly, and a large number of priests became obedient to the faith" (Acts 6:7).

The Jewish priests (i.e., rabbis) originally believed that the Christians were out of their minds. They rejected their preaching concerning Jesus. In fact, they took some of these preachers and put them in prison. They whipped them and disgraced them openly. But when the Word of God increased and people full of the Holy Spirit were taking responsibility, the priests could no longer deny the power of Jesus. And "a large number of them" accepted the gospel. That's what the power of the Holy Spirit does.

Many churches today wonder why their young people are straying into the world. At the same time, they have nothing but criticism for the Holy Spirit. Many parents are devastated when their young daughters don't come home on Saturday night, yet they keep criticizing the Holy Spirit.

The Holy Spirit gives us power to live the Christian life and to overcome sin. The Holy Spirit gives us power against the enemy of our souls. Stop criticizing the Holy Spirit and let Him do things the way He wants to do them.

When I was a boy in Ghana, I overheard some of my closest friends criticizing their Spirit-filled parents and other Christians. Like most children, I wanted to please the crowd, so I joined in. I criticized my own father and mother. I made fun of the laying on of hands and of speaking in tongues. Everyone laughed with me.

When I became born again and was filled with the Spirit, God reminded me of that behavior and convicted me, so I had to go to my parents and ask their forgiveness. "Daddy, Mama," I said, "if you were crazy for believing, receiving and acting on the leading of the Holy Spirit, then I have just joined you."

As I continued to grow, my family was so grateful to God that I had not become one of the wayward boys of the community. I have praised God many times for saving me from all the things the other boys my age were doing. I could have become involved in drugs and many other evil things. Thank God I entered into a life in the Holy Spirit and said, "Father, all I want to do with my life is to live it for You. I don't have time to play games. I mean business."

More than 30 years have gone by, but I still get excited about each new day. The Holy Spirit is a wonderful keeper, a wonderful guardian. I know that many good things are yet to come and I have never regretted my decision—even for one day—to serve the Lord and be a man of the Holy Spirit.

When sick people need my help, I call on that friend I met more than 30 years ago, and He always answers. When I say, "Jesus, I know that you love sick people, and I am believing you to heal this person," He reaches down in compassion and does the work. That's what the Holy Spirit does for you.

When I see blind people, I say, "God, look at them. You didn't intend for them to be blind. Oh God, open their eyes—in the name of Jesus." He often answers my prayer and opens their eyes. That's what the Holy Spirit will do for you.

Four times I have seen God raise the dead. One of those people raised was my own wife, Martha. As newlyweds, Martha and I traveled and ministered frequently in Mexico. One night in a packed meeting house, with Martha at my side as interpreter, I realized that she had ceased interpreting. As I turned to prompt her to continue, I saw that she had slumped over in the chair. Her eyes were rolled back in her head and she was limp and unconscious. Immediately, I prayed over her, rebuking the spirit of death. Just then, a doctor who happened to be attending the meeting rushed forward to the platform to offer his help. As we laid Martha down, he checked for her pulse and then looked up at me with tears streaming down his face as he shook his head no.

My dear wife was carried off and laid in the backseat of a car, while I calmed the crowd and quickly concluded the meeting. As soon as the meeting was over, I rushed to the car where I found Martha sitting up, dazed and disoriented but alive! The doctor was astounded by the tremendous miracle that the Lord had done, for he was certain that she was dead when they carried her from the platform. That's what the Holy Spirit can do for you.

Having experienced all this, should I now turn my back on the Holy Spirit and believe Satan's lies? Should I believe that the age of the Holy Spirit has passed and that the world has more to offer me now? Never! The world has nothing that interests me. I am dead to the world and alive in the Spirit of God.

If you want to walk in the power of God and see the working of the Holy Spirit, then get out of the influence of the world and into the Spirit. "Do not love the world or anything in the world. If anyone loves the world, the love of the Father is not in him" (1 John 2:15).

Jesus was gone when Stephen performed his miracles. Stephen could have said, "He's gone. The One we trusted is gone." But Stephen, like us today, knew the promises of God: Even if Jesus is gone physically, His power is with us through the Holy Spirit.

Jesus didn't say He would let the enemy ride roughshod over us. He said not to worry because He would never leave us: "And surely I am with you always, to the very end of the age" (Matt. 28:20). That presence is in the Holy Spirit. Don't reject Him!

God is still doing miracles through His people—by the Holy Spirit. People of God can still overcome the wicked one—by the Holy Spirit. Get involved! Don't be afraid of the Spirit of God.

How terrible that we don't hesitate to get close to Satan, but we hesitate to draw nearer to the Spirit of God!

Let Him do His work in you. Don't be held back by tradition. Let the Spirit have His way!

How terrible it is that people fear the Holy Spirit more than they fear Satan. How terrible that they revere Satan more than the Holy Spirit. How terrible that we don't hesitate to get close to Satan, but we hesitate to draw nearer to the Spirit of God! How terrible that we are more sensitive to what Satan wants of us than we are of the Spirit's will for our lives!

These sad truths are all the result of Satan's deceptions. He is busy, faithfully doing his work.

Several years ago a young man from Georgia came into the church I pastor. He was drunk. He sat in the front row and went to sleep, and his snoring began to disturb people. When I began preaching, he woke up, rose to his feet and tried to interrupt me. The Holy Spirit gave me the wisdom to deal with him. "If you will wait until I finish," I told him, "I will answer all your questions."

When I finished preaching, he was again deep in sleep. I was led of the Spirit to approach him. I pulled him to his feet and tried to shake him awake. I finally got him to put his hands up; he was still groggy.

When we laid hands on him, the power of the Holy Spirit touched him, and he was slain in the Spirit. He didn't know what was happening to him.

After he lay on the floor for a while, he got up, shook his head and shouted, "God is real!" His drunkenness was gone instantly. He was a new and sober man—totally set free. Afterward he went back to Georgia and proceeded to call me almost every day for a while. Then he decided to move to North Carolina so that he could attend our church and grow in the Lord.

That's what the Holy Spirit can do for you.

Long ago I made up my mind that no one would ever make me deny the power of the Holy Spirit. No way! With many people it happens so gradually they don't realize what is taking place.

An illiterate lady from East Africa was so anointed of the Lord that when the sick stood in the spot where she had been standing or touched something that she had recently touched, they were healed. When an American evangelist visited her country, someone told him about her. He was so impressed that he decided to take her to Europe and America and let people see what God was doing through her. In the process, pride crept in, the lady lost that glorious anointing and never recovered it.

I remember the story of a daughter of a Christian man who drew near to him one day, put her head on his chest and looked up into his eyes. "Daddy," she asked, "is God dead?"

The father was stunned. "Of course not," he answered. "God's not dead. Why would you ask me such a question?"

The sincerity of the little girl struck the man as she replied, "You act like He's dead. I never hear you praise Him anymore. I never hear you talk about His love anymore."

That's what's wrong with most of us in the Church. Non-Christians think God is dead because believers are so silent. Because many believers have denied the Holy Spirit, we think that God is not moving as He once did. It isn't God that is at fault. It is the fault of those who have neglected His Spirit.

When there was a spiritual need in the Church, the disciples didn't form committees to solve their problems. They looked for people full of the Holy Spirit. I understand why Satan tells people that this Holy Spirit business is crazy stuff. He knows that we can change the world with God's power—manifested through the Holy Spirit.

Make a firm commitment to God today to never be ashamed of His Spirit and to allow the Holy Spirit to totally control your life in every way. When you make that commitment, Satan becomes powerless to touch your life.

Pray for Truth

Dear Lord, I want to know Your Holy Spirit more intimately. I want to move in a new direction in my life, guided totally by the Holy Spirit. Lord, please help me to surrender my fears of what You might do in my life. Help me to see that the Holy Spirit is my friend, and as I yield to Him, You will use me to do Your will more effectively. Father, also help me to believe that through the Holy Spirit, You can do great works through me—not to glorify me, but to glorify You. I submit and yield to Your Spirit today, Lord, and pray that You will do Your works in and through me. In Jesus' precious name. Amen.

CHAPTER 8

God anointed Jesus of Nazareth with the Holy Spirit and power, and . . . he went around doing good and healing all who were under the power of the devil, because God was with him.

ACTS 10:38

LIE: "HEALING IS NOT FOR AN ENLIGHTENED AGE"

Satan is hell-bent on convincing people—Christians as well as the unsaved—that divine healing has no place in an enlightened society. Scores of people believe our society is too advanced for that—we are too well educated for that. Satan's tactic is to tell them that healing can be dismissed just as easily as if it were another superstition that uneducated people have held down through the centuries.

If I were Satan, I would tell people that sickness is just a normal part of life and that Christians should expect to be sick just as much as non-Christians.

I would tell people that sickness is actually a good thing because it causes them to be more humble. I would tell people that when they come to church sick, they should just accept it and thank God for it. They should declare: "Praise God Hallelujah! My arthritis has flared up, but thank God it makes me humble."

I would tell people that anyone who has a life-threatening disease shouldn't believe God for healing because if they pass on from here, they go to be with the Lord anyway.

If I were Satan, I would tell people that their bladder problems, rheumatism or diabetes should just be accepted as part of the cross that God wants them to bear. Some people say, "I'm on that journey, and I have to bear afflictions. The good Lord understands. The sicker I get, the closer I get to the Lord."

If God, our Father, who loves us as sons and daughters, would purposely make us sick, then we have no business following Him. Sickness is not of God. If it were of God, then Jesus would have come to Earth promoting sickness. He didn't. He went about destroying sickness.

If I were Satan, I would tell people that there are certain cases that God cannot heal. If the doctor cannot do anything, then no one can do anything. I would make people believe that AIDS is God's way of disciplining them and that God has sentenced them to death. I would tell people that if they get sick because of sin, God will never heal them—neither in this life nor in the life to come. would do everything in my power to make people feel unworthy of God's healing power in their lives.

I would tell people that there is nothing they can do about destruction or evil coming against them—that God has allowed such things to happen. "Whether it seems good or bad to you, accept it as from the Lord," I would lie.

I would lead people to misunderstand and misuse the biblical account of Job and would let them identify with Job. "I am like Job," some people say. "God is using this trial to train me." Train you for what?

When the devil wanted to hinder Job, God didn't give him a green light to destroy his servant. He said, "Go ahead, Satan, because Job will not worship you. He will not side with you. He will be faithful to Me" (see Job 2:1-6). God didn't expect Job to believe everything the devil said; He expected His servant to believe what His heavenly Father told him.

It was not God who afflicted Job but Satan. God granted Satan permission to test Job (see Job 2:6).

If I were Satan, I would tell you that healing is not for today, that the day of miracles is passed and that we are not to expect the same things experienced by the first-century Church.

This is a particularly vicious lie, for if the age of miracles is passed, then salvation by faith in the sacrifice of Jesus—that greatest of all miracles—is also passed. The age of miracles is not passed, and God is still saving and still healing.

> If the age of miracles is passed, then salvation by faith in the sacrifice of Jesus—that greatest of all miracles—is also passed.

Several years ago, when my oldest daughter, Anna-Kissel, was just a year old, she became very ill. She began to cry, and despite our best efforts to soothe her, she just kept on crying. When her diaper was changed, we found that she had severe constipation and was bleeding from the bowels.

I could have said that God wanted to teach us something or that He was using our child's suffering to make us humble or that this experience was good for our souls. But I knew that wasn't the case.

I said, "This is not from God. This is Satan's work." (Only the devil would afflict an innocent child.) I put my hands on that precious girl and said, "Devil, you know that you are trespassing. You know that you have no right to be in my house. Who asked you to come here? Get out."

My daughter looked up at me and smiled, and I said to my wife, "Honey, she's all right. Get a new diaper for her." When the diaper was in place, the child stood up and toddled off to play. She was healed and had no more discomfort or problems.

Some people would have said, "Perhaps the Lord was trying to teach you a lesson in some way."

Now think about that. My baby is sick and in pain. And God wants to teach me a lesson by that? If that is the case, then Jesus made a big mistake by preaching healing. The Gospels are full of accounts of His healing the sick:

News about him spread all over Syria, and people brought to him all who were ill with various diseases, those suffering severe pain, the demon-possessed, those having seizures, and the paralyzed, and he healed them (Matt. 4:24).

When evening came, many who were demon-possessed were brought to him, and he drove out the spirits with a word and healed all the sick (Matt. 8:16).

Aware of this, Jesus withdrew from that place. Many followed him, and he healed all their sick, warning them not to tell who he was (Matt. 12:15).

The devil doesn't want you to believe that God wants to heal *all*. He will do anything to convince you that your case is different and that God can't help you.

If I were Satan, I would present half-truths about healing. I would remind people how Brother or Sister So-and-So died without receiving miraculous healing from God. "Are you better than other believers?" I would ask. I would use this to cause division in the Church.

Get God's Word deep into your heart. Resist the lies of Satan, and receive the miracle God has for your life. Healing is for today, and God still loves to heal His children.

Pray for Truth

Dear God, I must admit that at times, I do not believe You will actually heal those for whom I pray. I have even laid hands on people, fully convinced in my mind that nothing would happen. Lord, please help my unbelief, and remind me that a person's healing—even my own—is not based on how hard I want the healing. Help me to remember that I am merely a vessel and that You can and will heal through me. Help me also, Lord, to surrender even those loved ones who do not receive a physical healing, knowing that in this life, we see through a glass darkly. But may You increase my faith, Lord, to believe that You are, indeed, Jehovah Rophi—my Healer. In the name of Jesus. Amen.

CHAPTER 9

In those days when the number of disciples was increasing, the Grecian Jews among them complained against the Hebraic Jews because their widows were being overlooked in the daily distribution of food.

ACTS 6:1

LIE:
"IT'S OK FOR CHRISTIANS TO MURMUR"

In *Works and Days,* Hesiod, the ancient Greek poet wrote, "Gossip i mischievous, light and easy to raise, but grievous to bear and har to get rid of. No gossip ever dies away entirely, if many people voic it: it too is a kind of divinity."[1]

I would agree. One of Satan's goals with the Church today the same as it was with the Early Church at Jerusalem: to cause go sip, dissatisfaction and murmuring among the people.

In the early days of the Church, Satan was jealous because th disciples had the power of God and were very joyful. He was jealou because they were growing and prospering. He was angry becau they had liberty, and he despised the excitement that he witnessed on their faces. He had to do something; his kingdom was suffering defeat.

He couldn't influence the apostles to engage in drunkenness or adultery, so he tried to discourage them through persecution. But that didn't work; persecution only strengthened the Church. He finally hit on a scheme: He would play on the sentiments of the people; he would exploit the racial differences in their midst; he would exploit the needs of the widows; he would cause the people to murmur.

Murmuring has been one of the most effective tools of the enemy down through the centuries. It takes many forms and occurs in all types of settings. There is too much murmuring among families, at church, among coworkers and between friends.

My heart goes out to young people today: teens, college students and young career types. So many of them have such great potential. But in far too many cases, instead of achieving their potential and being blessed of God, they are messed up and confused. Many of today's twenty-somethings have great jobs and make excellent money—but shortly after payday, they are broke. For others, their problems manifest through drug, alcohol or other addictions. Many of today's young people are deceived and are in total bondage to the devil.

A particular tragedy I see among teens and their parents today has to do with murmuring. As I travel and work among people in my city and other places, I see the following problem: A teenager is struggling with a drug problem or other bondage. When the teen confides in his or her parents (thinking that Mom and Dad will surely have an answer, lend a sympathetic ear, and offer constructive advice), the parents don't know what to do, so they go throughout their circle of loved ones, telling everyone about it. They go from relative to relative and friend to friend, murmuring about what bad children they have.

When the teen knows that Mom and Dad have gossiped the teen's problems around, he or she is crushed and confronts his or

It's time that parents stop murmuring about their child's problems and petition God to bring victory into their child's life.

her parents. "Mom, what's this all about? Dad, why did you tell everyone? You say you are Christians. You say you believe in God. I thought you were going to help me. What are you doing to help me? Nothing! All you do is talk about me. All you do about my problem is gossip."

Can you feel what that child is feeling? It's time that parents stop murmuring about their child's problems and petition God to bring victory into their child's life. First, they must see their child through God's eyes—with love and compassion. Then, they must pray and fast and seek His direction, *together* with the child, and provide the type of loving direction and support that is modeled by Christ.

The very same thing often happens when you go to a brother or sister in your church for help—or when you go to a pastor, elder, deacon or counselor of the church. Your brother or sister has no help to offer; all he or she can do is gossip about you to others. The person you sought out for counsel doesn't help you—he or she helps destroy you.

Oftentimes, murmuring is a result of competition, which is fueled by our insecurities and jealousies. Instead of helping one another and blessing one another, we compete against each other. We murmur and gossip about anything and everything in order to tear down the other person and make ourselves look bigger and better.

And Satan doesn't care whom he uses. He often uses mature people who are supposed to know better. Surprisingly, I often see "seasoned Christians" doing everything they can to smear the reputation of a young person—who just might be one of the future leaders of the church and society. It almost seems that the older person is saying "Let's get 'em!"

Satan is delighted with this, for if the people of the church are preoccupied with competing and murmuring against one another, God's power will not be manifested in that place. People may go through the routine of religion and move through some lifeless programs; but when they walk out the door, they are empty.

This type of dry, empty religion breaks God's heart. With all of its problems, with all of its idiosyncrasies, Christ still loves the Church: "Husbands, love your wives, just as Christ loved the church and gave himself up for her to make her holy, cleansing her by the washing with water through the word" (Eph. 5:25). He gave Himself for the Church—that is why Satan is so intent on destroying it. And one of the tools he uses most effectively is murmuring.

The Church in Jerusalem was increasing. The people should have been happy. They should have been rejoicing, but some of them found cause to murmur.

In this case (thank God), the apostles had the wisdom to deal with the problem (see Acts 6:1-7). If we let Him, God will give us the solutions. He will lead us by the Spirit to victory. But murmuring, if not contained, will destroy us.

When murmuring gets into a church, that church quickly becomes lukewarm. It cannot be on fire for God and continue to murmur. I personally know some churches that are so cold you could ice-skate in the aisles. When a servant of God is invited to speak in such a church (someone with a burning message on his

Even Satan doesn't like lukewarm people. If you are not totally committed to him, he is not happy with you either!

heart, someone who has waited on God in prayer and has heard from heaven), the response of the people is often negative.

This is too much for me, they are thinking as they sit there with their arms crossed. *We don't want him (or her) in our pulpit. He is too controversial—get him out of here!*

Those churches then wonder why they are not able to pay their bills or why they have so many problems. I don't wonder why; I know why. They are denying the most essential element in the church: the power of the Holy Spirit. They replace the power of God with personal ambition, competition and murmuring; and the church grows cold.

God doesn't want you to be lukewarm; lukewarm people make Him sick. He said He would spew them out of His mouth: "So, because you are lukewarm—neither hot nor cold—I am about to spit you out of my mouth" (Rev. 3:16).

Even Satan doesn't like lukewarm people. If you are not totally committed to him, he is not happy with you either! He will not rest until you are totally, completely turned away from God—miserable, lost and alone.

Many believers are one day here, the next day there. They are up one day, down the next. They are happy today, sad tomorrow. They go up and down more than a yo-yo.

It is time to stand firm. You cannot serve two masters. Would you like it if your husband or wife had another lover? How would that make you feel?

The Bible is so clear on this issue: "No one can serve two masters. Either he will hate the one and love the other, or he will be devoted to the one and despise the other. You cannot serve both God and Money" (Matt. 6:24).

How do you suppose the two masters would feel? No doubt one of them would say, "Look, you are taking advantage of me. You are not keeping your commitments. I can't let this continue." And the other master would feel the same way. Finally, because you pleased neither master, you would be left hanging. Then Satan would appear to "rescue" you. He would say, "Now that I have taken you back, you must do everything that I want. You were rejected by everyone, and I rescued you. Now you must obey me."

At this point you might try to give Satan his marching orders. You might say, "Get out!" But he will not be intimidated. "It's too late for that," he will say. "Now you are in my control."

Do you wonder how it happened? It probably started with murmuring. And a lukewarm heart is the result of murmuring. Israel's murmuring in the wilderness was remembered in New Testament times:

> And do not grumble, as some of them did—and were killed by the destroying angel. These things happened to them as examples and were written down as warnings for us, on whom the fulfillment of the ages has come. So, if you think you are standing firm, be careful that you don't fall! (1 Cor. 10:10-12)

God has good things in store for us, but we must stand strong against the enemy. We must take heed and avoid murmuring. Since the day I came to understand the work of the enemy, I have purposed in my heart to keep on fulfilling God's will for my life, regardless of what happens. I intend to keep on sharing the love of God and teaching His Word. I intend to keep on praying (in season and out). I intend to keep on giving myself totally to the Lord and living by faith the way He wants me to live. I intend to keep on serving to the best of my ability. I will not murmur against God—whatever others may do.

The Pharisees missed the blessing of God because they murmured about every perceived fault of Jesus and His disciples:

> But the Pharisees and the teachers of the law who belonged to their sect complained to his disciples, "Why do you eat and drink with tax collectors and 'sinners'?"(Luke 5:30).

> But the Pharisees and the teachers of the law muttered, "This man welcomes sinners and eats with them" (Luke 15:2).

Jesus forbade the disciples to grumble: "'Stop grumbling among yourselves,' Jesus answered" (John 6:43). The only time the word "murmur" is used in the book of Acts is in the case of the Grecian widows (see Acts 6). In that case, the Grecian Jews felt that the Hebraic Jews were overlooking the Grecian widows in the daily distribution of food. But the Jerusalem church dealt swiftly and effectively with the problem. Thus, the Jerusalem church grew, was blessed, prospered and reached out. It did not live out its life murmuring.

In first-century Jerusalem, one of the ways Satan tried to divide the Church was by race. He did all he could to inflame the differences between the Grecians and the Hebrews. The enemy is still using the tool of racism effectively all over the world—especially in first-world nations.

Lie: "It's OK for Christians to Murmur"   71

If I were Satan, I would convince church-going people that they can safely continue to live in their unspoken, underlying racism. And sadly, in most cases no one will challenge them. They believe that by sending missionaries to Africa, Asia and Latin America, they will more than cover up their true attitudes toward other races. Such a person thinks, *As long as I keep those unpopular sentiments hidden deep in my heart, I will be okay. After all, the third world needs our resources. Who else can they look to?*

As long as those resources flow, quiet bigotry will go unchallenged—for now. Accordingly, if I were Satan, I would cause people to forget that God is no respecter of persons: "For God does not show favoritism" (Rom. 2:11).

Another prime cause of murmuring and division in the Body of Christ is the fact that each believer has his own "pet doctrine." If I were Satan, I would make people believe that their particular pet doctrine is so important and world-changing that they must be willing to separate from all other brothers, if necessary, in order to maintain their doctrinal position.

Beloved, it is so much easier to separate than to work out our differences! Working out our differences demands maturity, patience and sacrifice. "Surely God would not expect those things of us," I would say if I were Satan.

But remember Jesus' high-priestly prayer, and be assured that racism, division and sectarian small-mindedness are *not* part of God's plan for us:

> I pray also for those who will believe in me through their message, that all of them may be one, Father, just as you are in me and I am in you. May they also be in us so that the world may believe that you have sent me. I have given them the glory that you gave me, that they may be one as we are one: I in them and you in me. May they be brought to complete unity to let the world know that you sent me and have loved them even as you have loved me (John 17:20-23).

Do not let Satan continue to bring division and pride into your heart. Recognize his schemes and seek the Father's love—He is waiting to forgive you and to heal your heart.

Pray for Truth
Precious Lord, I know that there are hidden, dark corners of my heart where I harbor feelings of superiority over other people groups and races. Create in me a pure heart, O God, and renew a steadfast spirit within me. Forgive me of all uncleanness and racism. Father, Your Word also says that You despise murmuring and gossip. Lord, help me to surrender my negative attitudes and words to You; cleanse me, Lord, of bitterness and complaining. And Lord, help me then to be a positive, Christlike influence on friends, family and coworkers.
In Your Son's precious name. Amen.

Note
1. Nina Tang, *My Favorite Quotes*, August 1998. http://www-hkn.eecs.berkeley.edu/~ntang/quotes.html (accessed August 9, 2001).

CHAPTER 10

It was he who gave some to be apostles, some to be prophets, some to be evangelists, and some to be pastors and teachers, to prepare God's people for works of service, so that the body of Christ may be built up until we all reach unity in the faith and in the knowledge of the Son of God and become mature, attaining to the whole measure of the fullness of Christ.

EPHESIANS 4:11-13

LIE:
"CHRISTIAN LEADERS ARE NOT TO BE TRUSTED"

Do not be mistaken: Satan recognizes the importance of Christian leaders. He knows that if he can make them stumble, many others will follow them. The enemy is working very hard to that end. He knows that without a good shepherd, the sheep will stray, so he is doing everything he can to destroy the reputation of good pastors.

If I were Satan, I would try to replace godly leaders with blind leaders of the blind: "If a blind man leads a blind man, both will fall into a pit" (Matt. 15:14).

If Satan has caused you to stumble because of something some hypocritical person did, I hope you can see how foolish that is.

I would place some of my own servants in every congregation to serve as hypocrites. Oftentimes, when newcomers visit a church, their attention is drawn to the hypocrites in the congregation—those who give them the cold shoulder or are overheard speaking gossip about another church member. *If every Christian is like that*, they think, *then I never want to serve God.*

Let me tell you something: If you turn away because of a hypocrite, then you are smaller than a hypocrite. If someone doesn't live right, it is not your concern—you don't have to worry about it. Jesus will deal with that person. Your allegiance and salvation is not with man. Your allegiance is with God.

I have heard people say, "I really want to do God's will, but do you remember that preacher that we had in here? All he talked about was money. I can't believe that was of God. That made me stumble."

Satan will always have someone around to make you stumble—if you let him. He has a host of hypocrites and glory seekers that he can use—if you fall for it.

He knows that if you don't stumble over some hypocrite, you'll be stronger to resist and you will have greater victory over sin. He also knows that if he can con you into stumbling, it will have a domino effect. Someone else will see you stumble and say, "See that! That's the reason I don't go to church. That's the reason I don't follow God. Did you hear him say last week that he loved God? Now look at him. What a hypocrite!"

If I were Satan, I would tell people, "You shouldn't believe anything pastors or evangelists say. There are so many bad ones, and you never know who is sincere and who isn't. They are all a bunch of thieves. Everyone knows that."

There may be some insincere Christian leaders and, yes, some of them may be crooks. But I don't have to worry about that. Their dishonesty will catch up with them; God will take care of them. I don't let the existence of hypocrites and insincere people hinder me.

Hypocritical leaders will give an account of their deeds. If they are God's true servants, God will deal with them. If they are Satan's servants, they will receive their pay as well. Don't worry about them—put them out of your mind.

Don't stumble because of something a man or woman did. You can trust the Lord as you remember that "God is not a man, that he should lie, nor a son of man, that he should change his mind" (Num. 23:19). Always remember His unwavering, unending faithfulness: "God, who has called you into fellowship with his Son Jesus Christ our Lord, is faithful" (1 Cor. 1:9).

Serve God. He will never hurt you. He will never let you down, nor will He ever take advantage of you. He loves you and is waiting for you with open arms.

If Satan has caused you to stumble because of something some hypocritical person did, I hope you can see how foolish that is. Rise above your bitterness and take the victory God has prepared for you.

If I were Satan, I would try to convince people that the failure of others is all God's fault. I would tell them not to blame people. I would convince them that God fails people sometimes—that He is not reliable, not to be trusted. I would tell them that sometimes God is very slow to act in defense of His own. "Don't put much trust in God," I would say. "Use your own head. Use some common sense."

I would cause people to ignore the assurances of Scripture: "God is not unjust; he will not forget your work and the love you have shown him as you have helped his people and continue to help them" (Heb. 6:10). As well, I would try to eradicate their memory on certain Scriptures: "Do not repay evil with evil or insult with insult, but with blessing, because to this you were called so that you may inherit a blessing" (1 Pet. 3:9).

I would sow confusion in the Church to destroy its power. I would sow a lack of confidence among brethren. I would sow suspicion and discord.

Satan does it well, for he is the author of confusion. On the other hand, "God is not a God of disorder but of peace" (1 Cor. 14:33).

If I were Satan, I would attack Christian leaders with all my strength. When a prominent leader fell in any way, I would rejoice and cause others to rejoice. I would print it in every newspaper and keep people talking about it by bringing it up again from time to time.

I would cause people to scrutinize ministers so carefully and with such mistrust that they would misunderstand their words and actions and would libel them with accusations of financial and sexual misconduct. I would cause people to mistake the anointing for arrogance and a desire to control other people. I would have others read sexual undertones into the normal expression of God's love in His servants.

We must join forces to resist these insidious attacks of Satan. He may be a master of deceit, but he is no match for the power of our God. We are more than conquerors through Christ. Rise up, saints of God. Put Satan in his place.

Pray for Truth

Mighty God, help me to respect and honor the Christian leaders in my life. Help me to pray for—and not prey on—my own pastor; to uphold him, honor him, protect him in prayer and grace. Lord, for-give me for gossiping about the pastor or critiquing his sermon as if it were a movie or sporting event. Dear Lord, help me to stand in the gap for Christian leaders and to lift them up. Show me tangible ways that I can undergird my pastor and show him my dedication and gratitude. In Jesus' name. Amen.

CHAPTER 11

But even if we or an angel from heaven should preach a gospel other than the one we preached to you, let him be eternally condemned.

GALATIANS 1:8

LIE:
"THERE IS MORE THAN ONE TRUE GOSPEL"

There lived an old woman who was very religious. A steadfast teetotaler, she never smoked or watched anything inappropriate on television. Each evening she would read five chapters from her Bible before going to sleep.

One night she dreamed that she had died and was standing before the Lord in heaven. The Lord said, "I do not know you; go away from Me." But the lady said, "But Lord, I attended church faithfully for 73 years. I read the Bible every night."

The Lord interrupted her and said, "Yes, you read the Gospels, but you did not *live* the gospel. You knew *about* Jesus, but you did not *know* Jesus."

The next morning, shaken to the core, the woman slowly rose, dropped to her knees next to her bed and, with tears in her eyes, asked Jesus to be her Savior. For 73 years as a churchgoer, she had never understood—had never been told!—that without Christ, religion is dead. She had been fed an empty gospel.

Satan spends a lot of time trying to make people forget the true gospel by giving them another gospel. Satan doesn't care if we are religious; nor does he care if we attend church consistently. He is only concerned that we don't obey the true gospel. He inspires some preachers to say, "God is so good that He would not make anyone go to hell—regardless of what they believe or the way they live. I can't believe that a good Lord would do that to His children. God will not do evil to anybody. God is so good that He will let everyone go to heaven."

Satan would have us ignore the true gospel: "The one who sows to please his sinful nature, from that nature will reap destruction; the one who sows to please the Spirit, from the Spirit will reap eternal life" (Gal. 6:8).

God doesn't send people to hell. Contrary to Satan's lies, people send themselves to hell. Don't believe another gospel.

Satan would love for preachers to ignore the most important aspects of the Word of God and concentrate on a social gospel. He tells people that the most important topic of the day is world peace, a new world order. He urges religious leaders to concentrate on it and preach it. If I were Satan, I would overly involve preachers in political activity to promote these lofty goals. That would keep them so busy they wouldn't have time to attend to other important Kingdom work.

I would tell preachers that it is more important to feed people physical food than spiritual food. Obviously, we are called to care for the orphans and widows and to help the poor. However, I would

If I were Satan, I would cause preachers to put forth as examples of true Christianity people who are morally good but who have made little commitment to God.

make sure pastors spent most of their time concerned with the food supply. If they tried to feed all the people Satan keeps in poverty, that would keep them so busy they wouldn't have time to preach repentance and deliverance through the blood of Jesus. A gospel that doesn't have power to deliver through the blood of Jesus is not of God. It is another gospel.

I would tell Christian leaders that they should just concentrate on education. I would lie to them and say, "If people were better educated, they would serve God." I would make sure that their time was taken up with education, so they wouldn't have time to preach the truth of the Word.

I would encourage preachers to fill their sermons with current events, book reviews and plenty of jokes to keep the sophisticated, intellectual and unspiritual entertained and interested. Since people are not willing to sit long in church anyway, that wouldn't leave preachers much time to tell the truth.

I would have preachers tell people that it isn't really necessary to publicly receive Jesus into their hearts. "Just be a good mate," I would have them preach. "That is all

God requires of you. Just love your family. Just love your neighbors. If you are loving and go to church sometimes, you will make it to heaven."

These are common lies of our enemy. The Bible declares: "Whoever acknowledges me before men, I will also acknowledge him before my Father in heaven" (Matt. 10:32).

But Satan has his own agenda, and many are following him.

If I were Satan, I would cause preachers to put forth as examples of true Christianity people who are morally good but who have made little commitment to God. I would use famous people as much as possible, such as Hollywood stars. That would assure a good audience, and people would be deceived into believing that the lifestyles of all famous people are acceptable.

I would use as examples of the Christian life people who don't even go to church and would say that they are better than many people who do attend regularly: "They don't drink, smoke or curse. The good Lord knows they love their neighbors and do many good deeds. They are excellent role models."

I would promote such people for office in the church. In this way, I would be telling everyone that all you need to do to go to heaven is be kind and good.

I want to declare to you through the pages of this book that you can love your neighbors and do good deeds and still go to hell—if you don't love Jesus and do His will. Stop believing the lies of Satan. God is still a holy God, and He is still looking for a holy people. Wake up to the tactics that Satan has mastered so well.

If I were Satan, I would slowly but surely eliminate the word "holiness" from the vocabulary of preachers. After all, the mention of holiness is offensive to many people, and the word has been abused and misused. I would cause people to forget what God said:

> Since we have these promises, dear friends, let us purify ourselves from everything that contaminates body and spirit, perfecting holiness out of reverence for God (2 Cor. 7:1).

Make every effort to live in peace with all men and to be holy; without holiness no one will see the Lord (Heb. 12:14).

Since Satan doesn't want people to "see the Lord," he certainly doesn't want them to live a holy life. Now we are told it is impossible to live a holy life, so most people have stopped trying to live right. "God doesn't even expect it" is the new gospel being preached.

But God hasn't changed. His will hasn't changed. His Word hasn't changed. And the truth of the gospel has not changed. Reject Satan's lies and live victoriously in Jesus Christ.

Pray for Truth

Dear Lord, help me to pursue and embrace the one true gospel: the gospel of Jesus Christ that preaches that salvation is found only through the life, death and resurrection of Your Son. Lord, protect me from the world's definitions of heaven, godliness and healthy living. Place a filter over my mind, and the minds of my loved ones, to keep out the polluted, false belief systems of the world, which embrace salvation through works, without Christ. Lord, may I also be a lighthouse to my family, my job and my neighborhood, so the lost may come to know You through my witness. In the name of Jesus I pray. Amen.

CHAPTER 12

*For the king trusts in the LORD; through the unfailing love of
the Most High he will not be shaken.*

PSALM 21:7

LIE:
"CHRISTIANS DON'T NEED TO MAKE A COMMITMENT TO GOD AND THE CHURCH"

No church is a refuge. You won't find a church that can save people.
Salvation is only by grace and through faith in Jesus Christ. He is
the Way, the Truth and the Life. And no one comes to the Father
but by Him. He said it Himself (see John 14:6). If I were Satan, I

would confuse commitment to a particular denomination or church with a commitment to God and *the Church* (i.e., the universal Body of believers in Jesus Christ).

If I were Satan, I would cause people to ignore the Bible's truth of how to be saved: "For it is by grace you have been saved, through faith—and this not from yourselves, it is the gift of God" (Eph. 2:8).

I would tell people that they can be saved by their good works. I would convince them that they have much to boast about, reminding them often of the good things they have done: "You always treat your neighbor right. You are a good person, and the Lord knows your heart. He remembers that you go to church twice a year without fail, and He knows that you have supported the missionary programs of the church."

On the contrary, God said: "Not by works, so that no one can boast" (Eph. 2:9).

Still, humans love to boast, and Satan loves it when they do. When men and women feel that they have something to boast about, they tend to lose concern about a commitment to God. They begin to feel that they are good enough, and they don't understand why spiritual fervor is necessary.

Jesus shows us the error of that kind of thinking:

As Jesus started on his way, a man ran up to him and fell on his knees before him. "Good teacher," he asked, "what must I do to inherit eternal life?" "Why do you call me good?" Jesus answered. "No one is good—except God alone. You know the commandments: 'Do not murder, do not commit adultery, do not steal, do not give false testimony, do not defraud, honor your father and mother.'" "Teacher," he declared, "all these I have kept since I was a boy." Jesus looked at him and loved him. "One thing you lack," He said. "Go, sell everything you have and give to the poor, and you will have treasure in heaven. Then come, follow me." At this the man's face fell. He went away sad, because he had great wealth (Mark 10:17-22).

When we read about this young man coming to Jesus, we can sense the sincerity of his desire to have "everlasting life." That day when Jesus mentioned the commandments, the surprising reply was, "All these I have kept since I was a boy." The rich young ruler had done it all. He was a good man; most people would have considered him to be exemplary. But Jesus told him he was lacking something and that he needed to make a full commitment to God. He needed to take up his cross and follow Jesus wholly. That thought made the man sad, for he had many possessions.

Satan will use anything to keep you from making a full commitment to God. Particularly in the affluent nations of the world, Satan wields the perfect tool: the fear of having to give up one's riches. This one fear keeps many from taking up their cross and following Jesus. What He said to the disciples that day should shake every first-world resident into making a full commitment to God:

> Jesus looked around and said to his disciples, "How hard it is for the rich to enter the kingdom of God!" The disciples were amazed at his words. But Jesus said again, "Children, how hard it is to enter the kingdom of God! It is easier for a camel to go through the eye of a needle than for a rich man to enter the kingdom of God." The disciples were even more amazed, and said to each other, "Who then can be saved?" Jesus looked at them and said, "With man this is impossible, but not with God; all things are possible with God" (Mark 10:23-27).

If I were Satan, I would use pride to keep believers from making a full commitment to God. Satan understands pride—it was pride that robbed him of his destiny (see Isa. 14:12-14). He is a master at using the technique on others.

If believers have money, Satan tries to make them feel proud. Many actually feel that as long as they have money, they don't need God.

If believers are beautiful, Satan tries to make them vain. Many actually feel that as long as they have physical attractiveness, they have no need of God.

When young believers get a little education, Satan tries to use it to cause them to be proud and to forget God. The educational system contributes to this pride by blocking out the truth that everything came from God and that nothing could exist without His Word. Many young people begin to feel that they don't need God or the Church.

Pride is a terrible thing. It is rebellion against God, and He cannot tolerate it: "I hate pride and arrogance, evil behavior and perverse speech" (Prov. 8:13). Proud people are headed for failure: "Pride goes before destruction, a haughty spirit before a fall" (Prov. 16:18).

There is altogether too much pride in the Church. Some people are too proud to go to the altar and confess their sins. They would rather maintain their pride than know the forgiveness of sin through Jesus Christ.

Some people are too proud to receive prayer when they are sick or in trouble. They would rather maintain their pride and go on suffering.

Others are too proud to seek the Holy Spirit. They would rather maintain their pride and go on living powerless lives.

Still other people are too proud to receive money from others. They would rather maintain their pride and remain in deprivation and need.

What do we have to be so proud of? What does it hurt us to admit our need? Is everyone else perfect except us? Think about it. Yet Satan uses this insidious sin of pride to keep people from making a complete commitment to God.

Don't be deceived by the enemy's lies. Total commitment is necessary in order for you to experience His blessings and divine protection. Jesus must be Lord of your life, and church cannot be a convenient part of your social life. God wants to rule your heart: If He cannot, then you cannot be part of His kingdom. You can't put God off anytime you feel like it. You must make Him Lord of all—at all times.

If I were Satan, I would do everything possible to stop believers from supporting the work of the Lord through their tithes and offerings. I would make the word "tithe" (which means the tenth of our income that belongs to God) a foreign word to many churchgoers. I would give them every reason not to tithe, and I would cause them to totally ignore the Word of God, which says:

> "Will a man rob God? Yet you rob me. But you ask, 'How do we rob you?' In tithes and offerings. You are under a curse—the whole nation of you—because you are robbing me. Bring the whole tithe into the storehouse, that there may be food in my house. Test me in this," says the LORD Almighty, "and see if I will not throw open the flood-

What do we have to be so proud of? What does it hurt us to admit our need?

gates of heaven and pour out so much blessing that you will not have room enough for it" (Mal. 3:8-10).

I would help people to justify their theft, knowing that in robbing God they are robbing themselves and robbing their churches. I would make them want all the blessings of the Christian life without accepting any of the responsibilities.

Not only would I make every effort to keep Christians from having a generous spirit, I would also try to convince them not to be so hospitable. I would say, "That's old fashioned—nobody expects that of you anymore." I would make them forget what the Bible teaches: "Share with God's people who are in need. Practice hospitality" (Rom. 12:13). Here are two other verses on hospitality that have impacted my life:

Do not forget to entertain strangers, for by so doing some people have entertained angels without knowing it (Heb. 13:2).

Offer hospitality to one another without grumbling (1 Pet. 4:9).

Pray for Truth

Dear God, am I committed? Do I love You more than my possessions? Are You truly Lord of my life? Sometimes I place other things above You, Father: my pride, lust, fear, materialism. Lord, come reign in my heart. Take over completely. Guide me and rule me completely. Help me to give up my idols so that I might worship You in purity and fullness. Father, forgive me for having a lukewarm faith, like the church at Laodicea. And let me think of others above myself, to serve others and honor others. Father, take first place in my life once again. I give it all to You, Lord. In Christ's name. Amen.

CHAPTER 13

Dear friend, I pray that you may enjoy good health and that all may go well with you, even as your soul is getting along well.

3 JOHN 1:2

LIE:
"POVERTY IS GOD'S PLAN FOR EVERY BELIEVER"

Satan is working overtime to make poverty and lack synonymous with holiness and goodness. One of his ploys is to make people believe that owning things is not spiritual, that having money is not consistent with holiness and that investments or savings are a sign of carnality.

If I were Satan, I would actually convince people that money in any form is an unnecessary evil. I would cause them to misquote the Scriptures, saying, "money is the root of all evil," when, in fact, the Scripture reads: "For *the love of* money is the root of all evil" (1 Tim. 6:10, *KJV,* emphasis mine).

If you don't believe it takes money to live the Christian life, go to a Christian bookstore, pick out a nice Bible and try to take it without paying for it!

In order to keep Christians poor, I would prevent them from getting the best jobs. To accomplish this I would convince Christians not to give their very best at work. I would make sure they used their boss's time to pray and read the Bible, causing nonbelieving coworkers to say, "They are too heavenly minded to be any earthly good!" I would make them very critical of their "unsaved" coworkers so they would be uncooperative and hard to get along with on the job.

I would do everything to make them arrive to work late and be the first to leave the office in the afternoon. I would give them every opportunity to call in sick to keep them from going to work at all. In short, I would make them unreliable employees. In this way I would be accomplishing three things: I would be keeping Christians and the Church poor; I would be destroying the testimony of the believers; I would be keeping many more people from accepting the faith.

I would make it a point to see that Christians were kept from buying houses. I would tell them that it is better not to own anything because Jesus is coming soon, and they need to keep their suitcases packed and ready for the flight to heaven.

I would convince Christians not to pay their bills on time, even if they did have the money. In this way I would help them to acquire bad credit, causing bankers to lose confidence in churches and their members.

I would cause Christians to be so "spiritual" that they would write bad checks "by faith" to the church, causing a good percentage of the income of the church to come back in bounced checks.

Do you see why Satan wants to keep you poor? He doesn't want you to have a good testimony. He doesn't want the Church to be able to do its work properly. He doesn't want you to be able to reach out to help meet the needs in the world.

In most cases, God wants you to prosper so that you can give more for the spread of the gospel, while Satan is determined to keep you poor. He will do anything to prevent the expansion of the Kingdom to other nations.

There is no way to get to Africa, Asia or Latin America without a ticket for an airplane. God's servants need sturdy and reliable vehicles to travel within national borders, and gasoline and spare parts for those vehicles. It takes money to buy all these things.

If you don't believe it takes money to live the Christian life, go to a Christian bookstore, pick out a nice Bible and try to take it without paying for it!

Go to the gasoline station. Tell them you are a servant of God and see if they will fill your tank for free.

Don't pay your rent for one month and see what your landlord does.

The next time you get a speeding ticket, just pray over it instead of paying the fine.

You will soon find out that money is an essential part of the Christian life. God wants you to have money to spread His Word; Satan wants to keep you poor.

The thing I don't understand is why poverty is so attractive to so many people. Being poor is nothing to brag about. Being poor is nothing to be happy about. Does being poor automatically mean you will be unhappy or that you are somehow out of God's will? Of course not. There are many godly people who, due to circumstances beyond their control, are not materially prosperous. But I am not talking about that. I am referring to those who would glorify poverty—actually seek it out—or those who are financially bad stewards, thinking that it is somehow godly or noble to be irresponsible with what God gives to us.

A perfect example of this type of financial—and spiritual—irresponsibility is found in the parable of the talents. If you recall, the rich landowner entrusts five talents, two talents and one talent, respectively, to three of his servants before departing on a journey. Upon his return he discovers that the first two servants have invested their talents wisely and have each doubled their money. But the third servant, afraid of losing his master's money, simply digs a hole in the ground and buries the one talent. Upon the master's return, he says to the third servant:

> You wicked, lazy servant! So you knew that I harvest where I have not sown and gather where I have not scattered seed? Well then, you should have put my money on deposit with the bankers, so that when I returned I would have received it back with interest. Take the talent from him and give it to the one who has the ten talents. For everyone who has will be given more, and he will have an abundance. Whoever does not have, even what he has will be taken from him (Matt. 25:26-29).

In this life, we are all entrusted with God-given talents and opportunities, and it is our responsibility to make the most of these things for God's glory. It is Satan's goal to make us waste our talents and opportunities: not to develop our minds and spirits to be sharp for God; to neglect the financial resources He places in our hands and to squander them through mismanagement and laziness.

Perhaps you are not destined to be financially prosperous. That is OK. But I guarantee you this: God's desire is for you to be spiritually prosperous, growing in Him, being a powerful witness to your world. Don't bury your "talent" in the ground, out of fear that God is a vindictive master who will punish you if you fail. Take risks for God! Even when you stumble, He will pick you up. Even when you fail, He will teach You a lesson so that you will succeed the next time.

Take God at His word. Resist the lies of the enemy, and move into God's richness so that you can be a part of the furtherance of the gospel in these last days.

Pray for Truth

Loving Father, there have been times when I have handled my finances in an irresponsible way. Forgive me, Lord, for squandering those resources and also for rationalizing my poor judgments by saying it is Your will. Lord, help me to develop the gifts and talents You have given to me to the best of my ability. In this way, I will be able to better glorify You and spread Your Word. And Father, please help me to surrender my finances to You so that I might use those resources to help fulfill the Great Commission. Lord, protect me from the attack of the enemy who is the author of spiritual and financial poverty. And help me to help others who do find themselves in a condition of poverty. In Jesus' name. Amen.

CHAPTER 14

If anyone does not know how to manage his own family,
how can he take care of God's Church?

1 TIMOTHY 3:5

LIE:
"MEN SHOULD FIRST LOOK AFTER THEIR OWN NEEDS"

Contrary to the romantic notions perpetuated in movies, warfare in the Middle Ages was not as chivalrous and exciting as one might think. Many times, the most successful form of warfare was the siege, which could go on for months—even years—at a time.

Robert the Bruce, the fourteenth-century Scottish king who helped expel the English invaders and secure Scotland's independence, hated siege warfare. He thought it was a boring, tedious, excruciatingly slow wartime tactic. He didn't have the patience for it!

But make no mistake about it: We are fighting an enemy who takes his time and understands the intricacies of siege warfare. And our enemy is pounding away, day after day, year after year, attempting to erode the walls of confidence and character that form the central citadel of every man's soul.

Fifty years ago the expression "deadbeat dad" was not even a part of our vocabulary. Today, of course, at least here in the United States, it is a common term referring to fathers who walk away from their parenting or child support responsibilities. Why is it that, for the most part, it is the man who is less responsible in marriage and parenting concerns than the woman?

If I were Satan, I would work especially hard on men. After all, I wouldn't want them to realize their true potential, and I certainly wouldn't want them to lead their families into the blessings of God.

I would convince some men to become totally consumed with their work. I would make them hopeless workaholics. I would make sure they were too busy to be a part of the upbringing of their children or to show interest in family interaction and growth.

I would interest men in antique cars, model airplanes, architectural designs and computer games—anything, even "innocent" hobbies—to keep them from family and church responsibilities.

I would make men love electronic gadgets and the remote control of their television set more than the Bible.

I would convince men that religion is only for the weak, the defeated, the oppressed and the very young or very old. I would make it difficult for them to pray for more than a few minutes at a time.

I would make men think that it was a worthy thing to relinquish their position as spiritual head of the family to their wives. I would be delighted when men neglected these responsibilities and women had to step in and take them over.

I would convince men that showing their emotions is a sign of weakness and that they should have a superficial relationship with

> True bravery
>
> is taking
>
> action—
>
> even when
>
> you are
>
> afraid to
>
> fail.

their family, their God and their fellow believers. And I would make them react very offensively when confronted with these sensitive issues.

I would cause men to love the golf course and tennis court more than the house of God. I would make them feel justified in staying home and sending the family to church. Many men expect their wives to be religious, to be committed to the church and to participate in its activities. At the same time, they are not religious, are not committed to the church and do not participate in its activities.

I would cause the mind of a man to dwell more on the lyrics of every sensual record and latest hit song rather than on the hymns of our fathers.

I would cause a man's loyalty to his national political leaders to be replaced by criticism and insult. God says: "I urge, then, first of all, that requests, prayers, intercession and thanksgiving be made for everyone—for kings and all those in authority, that we may live peaceful and quiet lives in all godliness and holiness" (1 Tim. 2:1-2).

Because I was born in a third-world country, I have a great appre-

ciation for America as a nation. Even though I have traveled exten-
sively in Europe, I can say that no nation compares to the greatness
of America. Yet I have noticed that many Americans take their liberty for granted. Instead of being grateful for their freedom, they seek
excessive independence, which results in criticism and disobedience
toward the authority of their elected and appointed officials. Many
are blinded to all the good in America and can only see the bad.

Men, there is a difference between admitting one's problems
and weaknesses one to another (see Jas. 5:16) and being a weak person. Frankly, a weak person is one who is dying inside but is too
proud to admit it to anyone else. Look at King David, considered a
biblical role model of strength and courage. Here is a man who had
to flee his own kingdom, having been betrayed and usurped by *his
own son*. In the Book of Psalms is the story of a distraught man:

> I waited patiently for the LORD; and He inclined to me, and
> heard my cry. He brought me up out of the pit of destruc-
> tion, out of the miry clay; and He set my feet upon a rock
> making my footsteps firm. And He put a new song in my
> mouth, a song of praise to our God; many will see and fear,
> and will trust in the LORD. Since I am afflicted and needy,
> let the Lord be mindful of me; thou art my help and my
> deliverer; do not delay, O my God (Ps. 40:1-3,17, *NASB*).

Though David felt distraught and weak, he knew the source of
his strength. Like David, we need to rise up and realize that God is
our tower and strength, and He will bring us up out of the pit of
destruction. And remember: It's not bravery unless you are scared.
Breaking out of old patterns and walking into your destiny (along
with its requirements and responsibilities) is frightening, but it is
OK to be scared. True bravery is taking action, even when you are
afraid to fail.

As you walk into a new life of action and commitment, you are
not alone; you have a helper and a deliverer. As well, seek out the

help and accountability of strong Christian brothers who are willing to be honest and vulnerable with you.

Let's rise up and cast off the works of darkness. God has a great destiny for every one of us. Take your rightful place in the Church and the community. Don't let Satan steal God's best from you any longer.

Pray for Truth

Dear God, You know that deep down, I have many fears. Father, I sometimes feel immobilized by my fears of failure; therefore, I do nothing. I want to be the person You created me to be, but I know I can't get there without taking some risks. Lord, give me the strength that I do not have; give me the courage I have never known; and give me the peace that You will not fail me. Lord, forgive me for hiding behind my hobbies or work to escape commitment to You and the Church. But rather than wallowing in condemnation, help me now to be a person of action—one step at a time. In His name. Amen.

CHAPTER 15

You say, "I am rich; I have acquired wealth and do not need a thing."
But you do not realize that you are wretched, pitiful,
poor, blind and naked.

REVELATION 3:17

LIE:
"PROSPERITY IS ONLY TO BE ENJOYED, NOT SHARED"

A decade ago the Church watched in amazement as Communism in eastern Europe and the former Soviet Union crumbled along with the demolition of the Berlin Wall. Since the early '90s, I believe the enemy has lulled the Church into a false sense of security, believing that she has triumphed at last, and can now rest.

If I were Satan, I would make Christians feel just as satisfied as the man whom Jesus described in one of His parables:

The ground of a certain rich man produced a good crop. He thought to himself, "What shall I do? I have no place to store my crops." Then he said, "This is what I'll do. I will tear down my barns and build bigger ones, and there I will store all my grain and my goods. And I'll say to myself, 'You have plenty of good things laid up for many years. Take life easy; eat, drink and be merry.'" But God said to him, "You fool! This very night your life will be demanded from you. Then who will get what you have prepared for yourself?" This is how it will be with anyone who stores up things for himself but is not rich toward God (Luke 12:16-21).

I would make the Church believe that all her missions over the years have earned her a special place in the heart of God so that her ticket to heaven is assured. She can relax now, be at ease and enjoy her prosperity. She has nothing to be concerned about. She can stop worrying about world evangelism and start indulging herself more.

I would make her believe she is truly God's gift to the world. I would instill a sense that her priorities supersede the needs of the poor, the widow and the orphan. Her own needs are more critical than those of the drug addict or the prostitute.

If I were Satan, I would occupy the Church with beautifying herself (i.e., bigger church buildings, more elaborate sound systems, etc.), rather than using her resources for spreading the gospel. I would instill in her an obsession with appearance, causing her to spend more time and money primping than on anything else.

I would do everything in my power to cause the Church to waste time, money and resources on dead-end causes. I would constantly point out the wrong problem and would raise up my own servants in her midst to give false direction to this end. I would cause the leaders of the Church to be so caught up with their own wants and desires and visions and plans that they could not see the needs of their own spouses and children.

I would make the Church in North America believe that its particular brand of Christianity is far superior to others—that it is actually "the apple of God's eye." I would encourage her to continue to export a mix of faith in God and Western culture. Thus the little "Western culture centers" she would be opening in many places (i.e., areas unhealthily influenced by Western culture) would have little resemblance to the true Church of the Lord Jesus Christ. Thinking that she was planting churches, she would be planting confusion among the peoples of the so-called third-world countries.

I would delude Christians into believing that God owes them for all their hard work and sacrifice. I wouldn't mind if the Church were rich—as long as all the money was spent on the wrong things. That would play into my hands. I could then convince believers that they had need of nothing, not even God. And I would lull them to sleep.

I would teach rich Christians to hoard the wealth that God had given to them, assuring them that God did not bless them with prosperity to win the world but that the prosperity came because the world

Satan attempts to occupy the Church with beautifying rather than using her resources for spreading the gospel.

owed it to them for their goodness. "Now," I would tell them, "it is time to kick back and enjoy life. You earned it; you are worth it. You deserve the very best."

I would cause them to ignore the Old Testament admonition:

When the LORD your God brings you into the land He swore to your fathers, to Abraham, Isaac and Jacob, to give you—a land with large, flourishing cities you did not build, houses filled with all kinds of good things you did not provide, wells you did not dig, and vineyards and olive groves you did not plant—then when you eat and are satisfied, be careful that you do not forget the LORD, who brought you out of Egypt, out of the land of slavery (Deut. 6:10-12).

I am sure you can agree that Satan has already mastered these tactics well. If you have been trapped by him, it is time to rise up and cast off the chains of bondage. Be free in the Lord Jesus.

Pray for Truth

O Lord, please forgive me for hoarding the wealth You have given to me. Though by Western standards I often think I don't have a lot (with my car payment, rent and credit-card debt), remind me that billions around the world do not even have enough to eat. But, Lord, help me not to wallow in pity or guilt but to take action—to rise up and inspire other Christians to heed Christ's words in Matthew 28 to go into all the world and make disciples. Father, please help me to break out of my self-centered world and lifestyle and to reach out—financially, physically and prayerfully—to those who do not know You. In Christ's precious name I pray. Amen.

CHAPTER 16

Do you not say, "Four months more and then the harvest?" I tell you, open your eyes and look at the fields! They are ripe for harvest.

J O H N   4 : 3 5

LIE:
"THE GREAT HARVEST IS JUST A MYTH"

Many in the Church today believe that the end-time harvest is close at hand. But if I were Satan, I would disguise the coming harvest—the greatest that God has ever prepared. I would cause even the elect of God to be fooled into believing that those who are hungry for truth are actually dangerous false religionists. Instead of embracing them and winning them, I would cause the elect to drive them away.

This is what I believe has happened with those who are members of what we call the New Age movement: The Church fasted, prayed and believed God for many years for a harvest. Then when

At some point, the Church will wake up and realize what is happening, but that may very well be too late.

tens of millions of people began searching through Eastern religions and mysticism, instead of the Church rising up in the power of the Holy Spirit and ministering the true gospel to these hungry people, the Church leaders panicked and proclaimed these people to be our worst enemies.

I believe most of these people represented little threat to Christianity; they were only intellectually searching for truth. I doubt the theory that there exists a great conspiracy intent among them to pull believers from their churches and damn their souls. If our people are well grounded in the Lord, nothing can pull them away from Christ, our guide and shepherd: "My sheep listen to my voice; I know them and they follow me" (John 10:27).

The purpose of Satan in all this is not only to disguise the harvest and pit us against the thirsty souls of our time but also to keep us occupied while the true enemy of Christianity takes up his position against us. For while we are thus occupied, a well-planned, well-financed assault is being made against us; and most of us don't even recognize it.

We have many forces assaulting the fabric of our culture today, including many false religions, paganism, racism and prejudice, and the list goes on. While we sit back, there are various militant groups striving to win the hearts and minds of our young people by diverting their attention to worldly matters. These groups have no love for the Christian Church and would like nothing more than to see its complete demise. That is why we must be aware of the enemy's schemes and to pray for those around the world who do not believe in Christ. Just as important, we must also have a ready witness to counter their claims that Christ is not the true Savior.

At some point, the Church will wake up and realize what is happening, but that may very well be too late. The harvest may, by then, be lost; and the enemy may be fully entrenched.

Satan is a master deceiver. Wake up, Church, before it is too late. Use your God-given wealth to reach out to the nations quickly, while there is time.

Pray for Truth

Loving God, thank You for the gift of faith and for our salvation, which is the most precious thing on Earth. Lord, help us to wake up to the fact that Satan does not want unbelievers discovering the beauty of salvation, as have born-again Christians. Reveal to me ways I can pray and act to alert the lost to the differences between other religions and Christianity. Arm me, Lord, beyond my human ability, to speak Your Word in boldness and love. And help me to know what to do in the battle for my nation's young people. Father, help me to be alert to Your timing and plan for the harvest, and help me to be a harvester. In Jesus' name. Amen.

PART III

YOUR WEAPONS AND YOUR DECISION

BEING READY AND WILLING
TO PUT ON GOD'S ARMOR,
ALLOWING HIM TO ARM
YOU AGAINST ANY BATTLE YOU
MIGHT FACE.

If God is for us, who can be against us?

R O M A N S   8 : 3 1

YOUR WEAPONS AGAINST SATAN

Satan's power is nothing compared to God's power. The Scriptures declare that God is for us and that because that is so, no one else can prosper against us (see Rom. 8:31; Isa. 54:17). With God on our side, we can conquer every foe; no demon can harm us. The devil himself will have to flee from our presence. But it doesn't just happen; there are some definite steps that you must take.

Once you have learned to recognize the work of the enemy, once you know him and his tactics, then you must arm yourself against him. You cannot wait until some moment of crisis. When Satan attacks, it is too late to prepare—you must prepare now. God has provided armor for you; put it on. God has provided weapons for you; learn to use them.

First, put on your defensive armor, as described in Ephesians 6: Gird your loins with truth and put on the breastplate of righteousness (v. 14); get your feet shod with the preparation of the gospel of peace (v. 15); pick up the shield of faith (v. 16).

When you secure your armor in place, begin to pick up some of your spiritual weapons.

OBEDIENCE

Obedience may not sound like a weapon, but it is. When you submit to God, He builds a hedge around you that protects you from the onslaught of the enemy: "Submit yourselves, then, to God. Resist the devil, and he will flee from you" (Jas. 4:7).

If your life is not submitted to the will of God, no weapon will work properly for you. It is God's power in you that makes every weapon effective.

When you submit to those who are placed by God in leadership over you, they will then "watch for you":

> Obey your leaders and submit to their authority. They keep watch over you as men who must give an account. Obey them so that their work will be a joy, not a burden, for that would be of no advantage to you (Heb. 13:17).

A child is defenseless in this world, but when that child is under the protection of a loving mother or father, he is shielded from the adversary. No enemy has a chance against protective parents.

A tiny bird, newly hatched from the egg, is totally defenseless. But if that tiny bird will stay in the nest, under the protection of its parents, it is less vulnerable to predatory attack. Commitment to God brings you under His protection and that of His servants.

Living a life of obedience and submission to God involves knowing His will for your life and doing His will. He may make His will known to you personally, or He may reveal it to you through your pastor or other leaders. Either way, don't be rebellious to what He is showing you. When you wander away from the Body, you become easy prey for the wolves of this world. Submit yourself for your own protection.

THE WORD OF GOD

When Paul wrote to the Ephesians about putting on the whole armor, the first weapon he mentioned (apart from the pieces of armor) was "the sword of the Spirit, which is the word of God" (Eph. 6:17). No weapon could be more important than the Word of God. The Bible is a powerful tool that God has given to us. Learn to use it wisely.

Throughout the first two millennia, and particularly before the invention of the printing press in the fifteenth century, we depended heavily upon learned clergy to open the Word of God and tell us God's will for our lives. But we are now living in a different day. God has blessed so many of us with the ability to read, and He has placed the Word of God in our hands. We are now responsible before God as individuals, and He expects us to go to the Book and find the truth for ourselves. He expects us to learn His ways for our-

If God could teach Peter, an uneducated fisherman, He can surely teach you.

selves. He expects us to arm ourselves. Get your weapons ready—don't dare face the enemy unarmed.

Read the Word of God for yourself. If God could teach Peter, an uneducated fisherman, He can surely teach you. Don't blame pastors or teachers for what they may or may not tell you. The time has come for you to hear God for yourself. The time has come for you to know what the Word of God says. God loves you and wants to make His Word real to you. Do your part.

THE BLOOD OF JESUS

The blood of Jesus is a powerful weapon against Satan. Of course, you must be sure that you are redeemed by His blood. If you have never been covered by the blood of Jesus, you are vulnerable and defenseless against the enemy.

Since we have now been justified by his blood, how much more shall we be saved from God's wrath through him! (Rom. 5:9).

In him we were also chosen, having been predestined according to the plan of him who works out everything in conformity with the purpose of his will (Eph. 1:11).

The blood of Jesus is the New Testament covenant, replacing the animal sacrifices of the Old Testament.

In the same way, after the supper he took the cup, saying, "This cup is the new covenant in my blood, which is poured out for you" (Luke 22:20).

In the same way, after supper he took the cup, saying, "This cup is the new covenant in my blood; do this, whenever you drink it, in remembrance of me" (1 Cor. 11:25).

This involves more than partaking of the Communion table. It involves partaking of Jesus:

Jesus said to them, "I tell you the truth, unless you eat the flesh of the Son of Man and drink his blood, you have no life in you. Whoever eats my flesh and drinks my blood has eternal life, and I will raise him up at the last day. For my flesh is real food and my blood is real drink. Whoever eats my flesh and drinks my blood remains in me, and I in him" (John 6:53-56).

It involves having "faith in his blood":

God presented him as a sacrifice of atonement, through faith in his blood. He did this to demonstrate his justice, because in his forbearance he had left the sins committed beforehand unpunished (Rom. 3:25).

Faith in the blood of Jesus working in our lives gives us a boldness before the throne of God and in the face of the enemy as well.

Therefore, brothers . . . we have confidence to enter the Most Holy Place by the blood of Jesus (Heb. 10:19).

They overcame him by the blood of the Lamb and by the word of their testimony; they did not love their lives so much as to shrink from death (Rev. 12:11).

Just as the death angel passed over the houses where the blood had been applied in Egypt, so the devil is powerless against us when we have the blood of Jesus applied to our hearts.

The work of redemption by the blood of Jesus may be a one-time event, but there is a need for the constant renewing of the application of the blood of Christ in our lives.

But if we walk in the light, as he is in the light, we have fellowship with one another, and the blood of Jesus, his Son, purifies us from all sin (1 John 1:7).

Don't neglect this powerful weapon. Use it well.

THE NAME OF JESUS

Demons tremble when the name of Jesus is mentioned. They believe in Him and fear Him. There are many ways to use the name of Jesus as an effective weapon.

Learn to Pray in the Name of Jesus

And I will do whatever you ask in my name, so that the Son may bring glory to the Father (John 14:13-14).

In that day you will no longer ask me anything. I tell you the truth, my Father will give you whatever you ask in my name (John 16:23-24).

Deal with Demons in the Name of Jesus

And these signs will accompany those who believe: In my name they will drive out demons; they will speak in new tongues; they will pick up snakes with their hands; and when they drink deadly poison, it will not hurt them at all; they will place their hands on sick people, and they will get well (Mark 16:17-18).

Finally Paul became so troubled that he turned around and said to the spirit, "In the name of Jesus Christ I command you to come out of her!" (Acts 16:18).

Minister with Healing in the Name of Jesus

Then Peter said, "Silver or gold I do not have, but what I have I give you. In the name of Jesus Christ of Nazareth, walk" (Acts 3:6).

By faith in the name of Jesus, this man whom you see and know was made strong. It is Jesus' name and the faith that comes through Him that has given this complete healing to him, as you can all see (Acts 3:16).

Then know this, you and all the people of Israel: It is by the name of Jesus Christ of Nazareth, whom you crucified but whom God raised from the dead, that this man stands before you healed (Acts 4:10).

Preach in the Name of Jesus

And repentance and forgiveness of sins will be preached in his name to all nations, beginning at Jerusalem (Luke 24:47).

But Barnabas took him and brought him to the apostles. He told them how Saul on his journey had seen the Lord and that the Lord had spoken to him, and how in Damascus he had preached fearlessly in the name of Jesus (Acts 9:27).

And he spake boldly in the name of the Lord Jesus, and disputed against the Grecians: but they went about to slay him (Acts 9:29, *KJV*).

Give Thanks in the Name of Jesus

Always giving thanks to God the Father for everything, in the name of our Lord Jesus Christ (Eph. 5:20).

Honor His Name as Holy and Above Every Other Name

He said to them, "When you pray, say: 'Father, hallowed be Thy name, your kingdom come'" (Luke 11:2).

Far above all rule and authority, power and dominion, and every title that can be given, not only in the present age but also in the one to come (Eph. 1:21).

Therefore God exalted him to the highest place and gave him the name that is above every name, that at the name of Jesus every knee should bow, in heaven and on earth and under the earth, and every tongue confess that Jesus Christ is Lord, to the glory of God the Father (Phil. 2:9-11).

Know That the Name of Jesus Elicits Fear in His Enemies

Then they called them in again and commanded them not to speak or teach at all in the name of Jesus (Acts 4:18).

When the disciples did not obey, the religious leaders were angry:

"We gave you strict orders not to teach in this name," he said. "Yet you have filled Jerusalem with your teaching and are determined to make us guilty of this man's blood" (Acts 5:28).

Again they commanded that this powerful name not be invoked:

His speech persuaded them. They called the apostles in and had them flogged. Then they ordered them not to speak in the name of Jesus, and let them go (Acts 5:40).

But the first-century disciples could not be silenced. They had learned to use the name of Jesus as an effective weapon and were not about to give it up. That name brought them victory over every enemy. It will do the same for you.

Personal Testimony

Your personal testimony is one of your most powerful weapons. Protect it. The fact that the Lord redeemed you from a past life of sin, changed your life totally and set you on the path of righteousness should cause every demon to fear. Always remember that "they overcame him by the blood of the Lamb and by the word of their testimony; they did not love their lives so much as to shrink from death" (Rev. 12:11).

When the devil approaches you, remind him of the grace of God in your life. Remind him of the pit from which you came. Remind him of God's love for you.

If your testimony is weak, Satan will remind you of that fact every time you get on your knees to pray. If you are an inconsistent Christian, Satan will use it against you every time. Don't give him the chance. Guard your testimony and use it effectively against him.

The Power of the Holy Spirit

Learn to use the power and authority of God that is in you by the Holy Spirit. Jesus revealed His authority over the devil when He said: "Get behind me, Satan!" (Matt. 16:23).

If Jesus is living in you and you have the authority of His name, if you are baptized in the Holy Spirit and you have His authority, you can command Satan in the same way Jesus did. Don't hesitate to take control of the situation. Don't stand idly by and watch him tear your family apart; don't stand by and watch your world crumble. Exercise your authority, and chase the devil from your life.

PRAYER

Effective prayer is a powerful weapon. Jesus spent whole nights in prayer so that He could defeat every enemy and go forth victoriously to fulfill His calling in life. The important thing is to become consistent in prayer and to PUSH—pray until something happens.

Don't give up. Seek and keep on seeking. Knock and keep on knocking. Ask and keep on asking. The promise of God is for all who will pay that price in prayer: "Ask and it will be given to you; seek and you will find; knock and the door will be opened to you" (Matt. 7:7).

Learn to pray more than a few moments at a time. Stay before the Father's throne until the answer comes, until you have victory over the wicked one.

EVANGELIZATION

Once you have learned to use these defensive weapons well, it is time to employ another tactic: the use of your offensive weapons. We must not just stand around warding off Satan's blows. We were destined to tear down his kingdom, to take back those who have been enslaved by his power and to show the world that our God reigns.

We can do this by taking the battle to the enemy. Go out onto his turf and use all your weapons to regain territory for our God. Face the enemy squarely and put him in his place: "He said to them, 'Go into all the world and preach the good news to all creation'" (Mark 16:15).

We have nothing to fear, for Jesus has promised to be with us in this offensive action: "And, lo, I am with you always, even unto the end of the world" (Matt. 28:20, *KJV*).

When the disciples obeyed this command of Jesus to go forth in offensive action against the enemy, He proved that His promise was true: "Then the disciples went out and preached everywhere, and the Lord worked with them and confirmed his word by the signs that accompanied it" (Mark 16:20).

His promise has not changed, so go forth into the battle. You are powerful in God, and your armor is invincible in battle; your weapons are sure. Stand up to the evil one—stand up and preserve what is rightfully yours. Maintain your place in God, and don't give the devil even one inch. That is God's Word: "And do not give the devil a foothold" (Eph. 4:27).

Why should Satan have his way with you? Why should he harm anything that is yours? God is for you! You are powerful in Him! He has given you power over all the power of the enemy! Take your stand *now*!

I have given you authority to trample on snakes and scorpions and to overcome all the power of the enemy; nothing will harm you (Luke 10:19).

Pray for Truth

Dear Lord, when will I lose my fear of the enemy? May it be today, Lord, as I now realize that if You are for me, who can be against me? As well, stronger is He who is in me than he who is in the world. Father, I surrender my fears and anxieties about being overcome by the enemy. Lord, reveal areas of my life where Satan has been allowed to gain a foothold, and give me the strength to repent and receive redemption. Break old habits, Lord, and cleanse me, my family and my home. May You reign in my life, and may I be obedient to use all the weapons of the faith to help advance the Kingdom in this hour. In Jesus' precious name. Amen.

CHAPTER 18

But if serving the LORD seems undesirable to you, then choose
for yourselves this day whom you will serve, whether the gods your
forefathers served beyond the River, or the gods of the Amorites,
in whose land you are living.

JOSHUA 24:15

YOUR DECISION TO JOIN THE BATTLE

You need God's help to overcome the enemy, but that is no problem. God is more than eager to help you. If you have an open heart, God will move in your life. If you really want Him to set you free from the power of Satan, He is ready to do it.

Maybe the enemy has been deceiving you into thinking it is OK to live in your sin and that it doesn't matter what you do in this life, because heaven is your home. Maybe you are one of those who says: "I'm heaven bound, and God knows my heart." You know your heart too, and you know that Satan's words are lies. Some things need to be put right in your life.

Maybe you are religious. You have done everything you know how to do but are still aware—deep down in your heart—that you are not right with God. God knows all about it and wants to set you free.

Maybe you have never experienced the power of God's forgiveness through the blood of Jesus, and you want to get right with Him. Don't be embarrassed by that. We all have to do it at some point in our lives. Don't be concerned with what others may think or say about it. It is between you and God—be excited to get on His side. Take time right now to ask Christ to be Lord of your life, inviting Him to be your Savior. He always says yes to those who invite Him in.

Be open and honest with God. Speak to Him from your heart. He understands.

Maybe the devil has deceived you and told you that God is not a healer. I want to tell you that healing is God's specialty.

Maybe the deceiver told you that God no longer baptizes people in the Holy Spirit. I want to assure you that He is still doing exactly that.

Overcoming Satan and his tricks demands a decision on your part. You must become intolerant of his deceit and stop allowing him to ride roughshod over your life. You must say, "Satan, I've had enough! I will not give in to you anymore. It's over for you. Don't play with me. You have no place in my life."

That isn't so hard, is it? But no one else can make the decision for you.

Aren't you tired of being tossed about by this lying thug? Do you enjoy being robbed and afflicted and cheated? Why not give God a chance with your life?

Just say, "Satan, your lies are ended! I have discovered what you want to do in my life, and I will never again be open to you. Satan, I know now how you paint a beautiful picture and make your ways so attractive. But it's all lies. I will never give in to you again. I want to serve God. He really loves me. He has good things for me. I am through with you forever. I am tired of being on your altar of sacrifice. I am tired of being your slave. I am going to serve God."

If you are ready to make that commitment to God, I want to you to pray. Please pray with me right now—wherever you find yourself at this moment—and mean business with God:

Father God, I thank You for allowing me to read the pages of this book and for my willingness to recognize the works of Satan. The devil has indeed lied to me, but I am determined never to again collaborate with such an enemy. I will never again take sides with him. I thank You for exposing the works of darkness. In this moment I use the authority of God vested in me and, in the name of Jesus, command that every work of Satan, every power of darkness that tries to invade the light of God's people, back off. In the name of the living God, I speak to every demon force and I say, by the authority of God's Word, "You will not prosper in my life as I make a decision in this moment to commit myself to the Lord. I come against sickness, disease and infirmity. I come against weakness. I come against everything that Satan has brought into my body in an attempt to destroy me and destroy my relationship with God. Back off! Take your hands off this child of God. You have no right to afflict me any longer. Lying spirits, I command you to flee in the name of Jesus." And Father, I ask You to lay Your hands upon me. Let the power of the Holy Spirit move from the top of my head down to the soles of my feet and make me completely free. Father, let Your glory come down upon me and drive away every evil force. As I finish reading these pages, may I go forth in Your liberating truth. Amen.

Friend, Jesus is making you free. In the name of Jesus, be free—in spirit, soul and body. The enemies of God have rejoiced over you too long. Be free. Now the angels of heaven will rejoice over your liberation. Every lie from Satan is now broken. Be free! In Jesus' name, be free!

Amen!

Resources by
DR. KINGSLEY FLETCHER

BOOKS

I Have Seen the Kingdom
After years of democracy and free will, has America lost sight of the biblical views of the kingdom of God? Pastor and teacher Kingsley Fletcher brings his own experience as the son of a king in Ghana, West Africa, to this book, giving us insight to tapping into the glory of God through the understanding of Kingdom principles.

Prayer and Fasting
Fasting and prayer will sharpen your expectancy so that when you ask, you expect to receive. Discover the benefits of prayer and fasting and how to fast effectively. A practical guide to a lifestyle of prayer and fasting explaining the preparation, the purpose, the action and the anticipated results.

The Power of Covenant
We live and die by our relationships, beginning with the covenants we make with God and others. Kingsley Fletcher brilliantly reveals covenant principles and explains their priority to God. The power of covenant must be applied to our daily lives and the life of the Church. Learn how our covenants with God bind us together forever in our friendships, marriages and, ultimately, to God Himself.

Catch on Fire!
Telling others about God is at the very heart of the Christian life. Re-ignite the fire of your salvation and learn how to bring others into salvation. Tremendous teaching on evangelism for our times.

AUDIOCASSETTES

Prayer and Fasting

Four-part cassette series outlining the preparation, purpose, results and action of prayer and fasting. Tremendous companion to book on this subject. Contains information not included in the book.

A Place Called There

There is a special place in God that not everyone has access to—the secret places of the Lord. Learn how to tap into it and advance in Him! Two cassettes.

Covenant Relationships

Six-cassette study on the promises given to Abraham with explanation on how they carry on to us. God has obligated Himself to fulfill His covenant promises. He desires to bless us. Foundation tapes for the book. Revealing study.

How to Win in Spiritual Warfare

You *can* be victorious and triumphant in spiritual battles! Learn to identify the spiritual forces attacking you and learn to come against the real enemy with power. Four cassettes. Life changing!

Walking in Divine Favor

God desires to favor us as His children. There are three necessary components to His favor: the attitude of the heart, honoring the Lord and maintaining faithfulness. God has more than enough and desires to bless you. Learn how to walk in His favor and receive the blessings he bestows.

The Grace of Giving

The law of reciprocity is at work in all areas of the Kingdom: Give and it shall be given unto you. Learn the Kingdom truth at work in this law. God gave us his BEST—His Son; and in so doing has reaped a harvest of sons. Christ gave His LIFE—that we may live. Discover how to direct YOUR seed as you plant it and allow break-through to flow in your life.

Five Things That Lead to the Presence of God
Moses asked God to show him His glory. His presence was not enough; Moses wanted the glory as well. Your ultimate desire of God should also be to experience His presence and His glory. Enter into His presence and you will discover true peace and joy.

Gifts, Talents, Abilities and Skills
In addition to filling us with His Holy Spirit, God endows us with talents, abilities and skills for the advancement of His kingdom. Learn to identify your special gifts and see how you can advance in both the spiritual and natural kingdoms by putting them to proper use.

Keys to Your Success
When we learn the principles of success given in the Word, we can apply them to our daily lives. *"I wish that in all ways you would prosper and be in good health."* Valuable to your spiritual and natural walk. Six cassettes.

Transference of Spirits
Five-cassette series enlightening us to understand the different kinds of spirits that affect our daily lives and our walk with God. Spirits can be transferred. Make certain you open yourself up only to those you wish to influence your life!

Jesus First!
"Seek ye first the kingdom of God and His righteousness . . ." Learn how placing Jesus first opens us up to all the promises of God. Simple, relevant teaching that gives insight to the joy of serving Him and walking in right relationship with Him. Two cassettes.

Experiencing God's Power

Be consumed with the zeal of the Lord and experience His power in your life! Those that know the Lord will do exploits in His name. Ignite everything in your path. Two cassettes.

Living and Walking in God's Power

Learn through practical experience how to walk and live in His power in all aspects of your life. A must for all believers! Two cassettes.

*For more information about these
and other resources by Kingsley Fletcher or to
place an order, write or call:*

KINGSLEY FLETCHER MINISTRIES

P. O. BOX 12017
RESEARCH TRIANGLE PARK, NC 27709-2017
PHONE: (919) 382-1944
WEBSITE: WWW.KFMLIFE.ORG